ELIJAH AND ELISHA IN SOCIOLITERARY PERSPECTIVE

**THE SOCIETY OF BIBLICAL LITERATURE
SEMEIA STUDIES**
Edward L. Greenstein, Editor

ELIJAH AND ELISHA
IN SOCIOLITERARY PERSPECTIVE

Edited by
Robert B. Coote

Scholars Press
Atlanta, Georgia

ELIJAH AND ELISHA
IN SOCIOLITERARY PERSPECTIVE

© 1992
The Society of Biblical Literature

The Lenski diagram on page 6 is reprinted from *Power and Privilege: A Theory of Social Stratification,* by Gerhard Lenski. Chapel Hill: The University of North Carolina Press, 1984.

Library of Congress Cataloging in Publication Data

Elijah and Elisha in socioliterary perspective / edited by Robert B. Coote.
    p. cm. — (Semeia studies)
    Includes bibliographical references and indexes.
    Contents: The pre-Deuteronomistic Elijah cycle / Judith A. Todd— The local hero in Palestine in comparative perspective / Scott D. Hill — The Elijah-Elisha stories / Tamis Hoover Renteria — The prophetic alternative / Wesley J. Bergen.
    ISBN 1-55540-708-0 (alk. paper). — ISBN 1-55540-709-9 (pbk.)
    1. Elijah (Biblical prophet) 2. Elisha (Biblical prophet)
I. Coote, Robert B., 1944- . II. Series.
BS580.E4E42 1992
222'.506—dc20   92-5254
                                                          CIP

Printed in the United States of America
on acid-free paper

Contents

Introduction
    Robert B. Coote ix

1. The Pre-Deuteronomistic Elijah Cycle
    Judith A. Todd 1

2. The Local Hero in Palestine in Comparative Perspective
    Scott D. Hill 37

3. The Elijah/Elisha Stories:
   A Socio-cultural Analysis of Prophets and People
   in Ninth-Century B.C.E. Israel
    Tamis Hoover Rentería 75

4. The Prophetic Alternative: Elisha and
   the Israelite Monarchy
    Wesley J. Bergen 127

Works Cited 139

Subject Index 151

Author Index 155

Contributors

WESLEY J. BERGEN is a graduate of Swift Current Bible Institute, the University of Manitoba, and Lutheran Theological Seminary and St. Andrews College in Saskatoon. He is currently a Th.D. candidate in Old Testament at Emmanuel College, University of Toronto.

ROBERT B. COOTE is Professor of Old Testament at San Francisco Theological Seminary and the Graduate Theological Union, and author of books and articles on the sociopolitical meaning of biblical literature.

SCOTT D. HILL received his Master of Divinity degree from San Francisco Theological Seminary in 1990. He has taught in Cairo and Assiut, Egypt, and worked in Jerusalem and the Occupied West Bank. He is currently teaching English as a second language in Rabat, Morocco.

TAMIS HOOVER RENTERÍA received her M.A. in biblical studies from the Graduate Theological Union in 1984, and from Stanford a B.A. in 1978 and an M.A. in 1986, both in anthropology. She is a candidate for the Ph.D. in anthropology at Stanford.

JUDITH A. TODD is Visiting Assistant Professor of Biblical Studies at Central Baptist Theological Seminary in Kansas City, Kansas. She received her Master of Divinity degree from McCormick Seminary in 1975 and her M.A. in biblical studies from the Graduate Theological Union in 1982. She received her Ph.D. in Old Testament from the Graduate Theological Union in 1990. She has taught courses in Bible, Hebrew, and Greek in the San Francisco Bay area, and is author of several studies, including "Remember and Go Forth," the 1986-87 study on covenant for Presbyterian women.

Introduction

ROBERT B. COOTE

The four essays in this collection address the social nature of Elijah and Elisha and the social nature of the biblical narratives about them, from four related perspectives. The essays progress from the nature and purpose of the text pertaining to Elijah in its present form, to the generic role represented by Elijah and Elisha, to the nature of the individual stories, oral and written, about both, but particularly Elisha.

Throughout an attempt is made to relate literature to the social realities of ninth century B.C.E. Israel. Todd's essay presents a close analysis of the language and structure of the Elijah stories in 1 Kings 17–19, the centerpiece of her argument, and shows that, together with 1 Kings 21, 2 Kings 1, and 2 Kgs 2:1–18 (three independent units linking Elijah's tie to Elisha to later episodes involving Elisha), they form a composition crafted almost entirely on the basis of the Elisha stories that follow. It then becomes evident, from structure and rhetoric, that in its pre-Deuteronomistic form the Elijah cycle, pivoting on the commission to Elijah and Elisha in 1 Kings 19, was composed to compound support for Jehu's coup d'état against the House of Omri, by some Jehuid if not Jehu himself. In this sense, Todd's work represents an extension of the brilliant analysis of chiefly the Elisha narratives by Rofé (1988, 1989).

Todd's discussion does not detail the chronology of composition. However, as shown again recently by Rofé (1988:70–74) and others, at least several of the original Elisha stories must be dated in the time of Jehu and his successors Joahaz and probably Joash, rather than in the time of the Omrids, as suggested by Todd. Thus the generic folk stories as described by Rentería and the history of oppression they reflect, under the Jehuids no less than the Omrids, serve in their present form of presentation the political aim of the house of Jehu to justify their usurpation a generation or more after the event, and to relate that usurpation to the rule of Hazael, who made such deep inroads in Palestine during the first generation of the house of Jehu's rule. Such legitimating aims are characteristic of much of what makes up the Torah and Prophets.

Todd's close reading, while stimulatingly naive when compared with many more sophisticated structuralist treatments, may at first appear to contradict the narrative sense of verbal and rhetorical simplicity developed by Rentería, an impression perhaps strengthened by the synchronic focus of Todd's textual analysis in contrast to Rentería's historical focus. As Greenstein has pointed out, however, the multidimensional biblical text invites both kinds of reading simultaneously (Greenstein, 1988:352–53; 1989:69–72). Moreover, the studies of Todd and Rentería, excepting one or two of their examples, point up once again that with Elijah and Elisha we are probably dealing with two quite different types of tradition. The Elijah narratives are more closely related to literate scribes' purposes, whereas the Elisha narratives in general appear more dependent on the voices of oral folk narrative. The frequent and studied allusion to Moses in the Elijah narratives, much less characteristic of the Elisha narratives, may be based on literary imitation and hence seems to point in the same direction.

Hill's essay makes a pioneering attempt to delineate the probable social role of the historical individuals behind the portrayals of Elijah and Elisha. However, rather than placing weight on an investigation of these particular figures through the narratives about them, Hill analyzes the disparate and difficult data available regarding ostensibly similar figures in other periods of Palestinian and Middle Eastern history, leaving his intentionally general comments about Elijah and Elisha to the end of his discussion. There are many pitfalls in such a comparative study, which Hill takes great care to avoid. In the end he presents not a single portrait of "the prophet" (local hero in his terminology), but a complex and shifting set of parameters, which suggest an explanatory matrix requiring further definition. The parameters Hill suggests center on a community's use of truth and power, which typically characterize such figures.

Hill deals little with Elijah and Elisha directly. The application of his results to these figures is mostly by implication, in keeping with the intentional indirection of his method. (Rentería's essay makes further applications). The potential frustration readers may feel with this essay thus has real causes, but they should not be laid at Hill's feet. The terminological issue with which Hill begins focuses the essential problem: we have an abundance of terminology for the social role we are looking at, but at the same time a dearth of experience and understanding of what is a genuinely alien social reality, in which among other things the distinction between living and dead carries little if any significance. Hill's foray into this strange territory—or, better put, territory whose strangeness we would do well to rediscover—is essentially heuristic, pointing forward to understandings beyond his own and ours. This cannot be done without risk.

While there have been many studies of nonbiblical prophets of relevance to the biblical prophets, Hill's study may be unique in its attempt to integrate and make sense of the whole panoply of evidence with some geographical or historical connection to Palestine. The usefulness of this perspective is bound to become more apparent, as more recent studies of *welys*, studies exemplified by Reeves' masterful analysis (1990), come to the attention of biblical scholars. Such studies will go a long way in helping to locate such discussions as Rofé's excellent treatment of the legends and relics of biblical holy men (Rofé 1988:22–26), already suggestively comparative, within a wider interpretive framework.

Rentería's essay places the stories of Elijah and Elisha as folk narrative in the context of the oppression of primarily the village class by the Omrids, and presumably by the Jehuids as well, brought about in large part by the commercialization and militarization of political, i.e. elite, Israel during the ninth century. Like Hill, Rentería respects the particularity of her subject while taking advantage of the insights to be gained through careful comparative study. Rentería's goal is to discover the lived experience of the people who told the stories about Elijah and Elisha. Her social analysis of such storytellers is probably more precise than any other currently available.

Rentería's method is based on recent work in anthropology sensitive not only to the historical dynamics supposed to have characterized Omrid and Jehuid society, but also finely tuned to the ambiguities and snares of interpreting cultural information, the critical problems of anthropological method of importance to the field today. While bringing the sophistication of anthropological discipline to bear on her subject, Rentería at the same time succeeds in conveying its troubling poignancy.

Bergen's essay explores the ideological subtext that undergirds, or undermines, the touting of Elisha in the biblical text. The prophet as a potential leader of an alternative political formation must be limited by and subordinated to the inevitable requirements of the institution of monarchy. For the Deuteronomist and probably for his scribal predecessors, Elisha stands for Moses and the authority of Moses, representing in theory a power greater than the king. The text, as a king's text, therefore has the task of portraying the prophet as God's legitimate spokesperson while at the same time preventing the prophet from intruding upon monarchic power. The importance of this task could hardly be overstated. If the writer had not succeeded, we would not have the text today.

The social historian must, however, be especially sensitive to the literary methods of the dominant voice in the narrative, which obscures one social reality (or several such realities) while obliquely expressing another—both realities essential to a full understanding of the text. Bergen is particularly interested in ways in which inconsistencies in the text may reflect inconsistencies within the ideology that dominates the text. "The coming of Elisha," Bergen suggests, "proves to be the place where the veneer of ideological coherence is unable to hide the basic flaws underneath." This discussion thus provides an example of an important dimension of current socioliterary studies of the Hebrew Bible.

These essays join the debate over the relation between literary and sociohistorical studies of the Bible at a critical juncture. The relation between the two approaches continues to be quite uncertain, despite recent attempts to define such a relation. The question remains: do these approaches intersect or not? Greenstein's point is correct: they may or may not intersect, either way with justification. If, however, they are to intersect constructively, then perhaps they must follow the example of these essays, in grounding the dual vision required for biblical interpretation in our time in an awareness of the devices of power—politics in a word—and then explaining those devices in terms of an analysis of structure, rhetoric, and history that is systemic and comparative. Why the devices of power? Because power, whether broadly or narrowly understood, was the root use of writing. This is the necessary point of intersection, and this is what we are offered in the collective effort contained in this book.

As already hinted, these essays are not put forward as definitive treatments. They represent preliminary endeavors to take the resources of social understanding seriously and, in applying them to the well-defined subject of Elijah and Elisha, to influence the categories with which these prophets and their stories may in the future be approached. The essays are short, but make their points no less effectively for that. They will be found accessible to beginning Bible students as well as experts, and have already proven useful in the seminary and graduate classroom. To have them together in one place, where readers can share their insights through the effort merely of reading this slim volume, should prove a boon to students, teachers, and researchers alike.

❧ 1 ❧

The Pre-Deuteronomistic Elijah Cycle

JUDITH A. TODD

Introduction

Prophets speak to specific situations in their society. Elijah spoke the word of Yahweh in a society confused by conflicting religious claims, and Elisha, his successor, encouraged a revolt against the ruling "house of Ahab." Legends about these prophets circulated within the society and conveyed their authoritative words to the disenfranchised.

Within the Deuteronomistic History's account of the period of the Omrid dynasty and the Jehu revolution which overthrew it (1 Kgs 16:15–2 Kgs 13) is a cycle of Elijah-Elisha stories that give voice to the traditional values that were under pressure from the socio-economic policies of the state. This cycle of stories was constructed in a way that gave legitimacy "without any doubt" to Jehu's reign in Israel. The legends of Elijah's opposition to Ahab, but mostly toward Jezebel and her Baal entourage, fueled the factions that opposed the "house of Ahab." The work of Elisha among the "sons of the prophets" fomented the rebellion against Joram's rule and brought events to a crisis point. The stories demonstrated physical refuge and sustenance for bands of people who had been forced out of the old protective tribal structures by the monarchy and social stratification. They also provided an ideological and organizational base for advocating Yahwistic socio-ethical concepts throughout the society on all levels. At an appropriate time after Jehu's rebellion, the legends were pulled together into a written cycle to authenticate Elisha's prophetic role in the revolution as well as the revolution itself.

The focus of this essay is on the literary units in which the prophet Elijah plays a part. Those stories are found in 1 Kgs 17–19; 21; 2 Kgs 1; and 2:1–18. The premise developed here is that the Elijah narratives are composites of oral folk tales that have been brought together for a reason. The written cycle is complex and can be discerned through an examination of its narrative design, which shows that there is a written level that includes all the Elijah stories. Although the secondary literature has rearranged the Elijah material in a variety of ways, it is not the intent of this essay to review that literature, but to present a new configuration of the data.

The Elijah stories are contained in six chapters and can be divided into two basic units of three chapters each. 1 Kgs 17–19 contain a set of Elijah stories illustrating three facets of Elijah's career, presenting his authority in his role as prophetic mediator. The second unit is made up of three independent chapters: 1 Kgs 21, 2 Kgs 1, and 2 Kgs 2:1–18. They pertain to the commission given Elijah in 1 Kgs 19:15–16 and tie together Elijah and Elisha's functions and authority:

> Yahweh said to [Elijah], "Go, return on your way to the wilderness of Damascus; and when you arrive, you shall anoint Hazael to be king over Syria (see 2 Kgs 8:7–15);
>
> and Jehu the son of Nimshi you shall anoint to be king over Israel (see 2 Kgs 9);
>
> and Elisha the son of Shaphat of Abel-meholah you shall anoint to be prophet in your place (see 2 Kgs 2).

2 Kgs 2:1–18 tells of the transfer of power from Elijah to Elisha and establishes Elisha as the unquestioned successor to Elijah's authority. 2 Kgs 1 illustrates Elijah's mediative power over life and death as it relates to a king, connecting with 2 Kgs 8:7–15, where Elisha mediates a similar power promoting Hazael as king over Syria. 1 Kgs 21 tells of Ahab's acquisition of Naboth's vineyard, an important location for Jehu's seizure of power in 2 Kgs 9. In this way, Elisha's actions were closely tied to Elijah traditions and were written down to authenticate both Elisha's prophetic support and the legitimacy of the Jehu revolution.

Because the purpose of this written pre-Deuteronomistic Elijah/Elisha cycle was to speak authoritatively in legitimating a social reality, section 1 will explore the context for the Jehu revolution. Political and socio-economic pressures increased tensions within the stratification of society during the period under study. As these tensions corresponded to an increased syncretism within the religious sphere, the prophets spoke and acted against the ruling dynasty. Section 2 will concentrate on 1 Kgs 17–19, the first unit of Elijah stories, through an examination of the Hebrew rhetorical devices found there, with the assumption that these devices were used as deliberate techniques. This methodology allows entry into the world of the internal emphases in the text, giving clues to the structural intention of the narrative. Section 3 will analyze the relationships between Yahweh's commission to Elijah at Mt. Horeb and the second set of three Elijah stories with their matching Elisha units. This analysis will demonstrate that all the Elijah stories are part of a cycle that has internal cohesiveness and method in its presentation.

1. The Socio-Economic Context of the Omrid Dynasty

The social history of the rise and demise of the Omrid dynasty provides the context in which the Elijah cycle was constructed. The economy of the Omrid dynasty fits into a typical "advanced agrarian" model, consisting of a rural-based agricultural sector and an urban-based commercial and industrial sector (Lenski and Lenski: 201). The political and economic policies of the rulers (Omri, Ahab, Ahaziah, and Joram) supported a social stratification that increased the asymmetrical structural relationship between those who produced a surplus from the land (the peasantry) and those who controlled the use of that surplus (the elite). Gerhard Lenski has identified two laws of distribution of goods in a society; the first deals with distribution for survival, the second with any surplus. As any surplus will give rise to conflict aimed at its control, "power will determine the distribution of nearly all the surplus possessed by a society" (Lenski: 44). As societies move from hunting and gathering, through horticultural, and into agrarian activities, an increasing proportion of the goods and services available will be distributed on the basis of power. In the Israelite society of this period, the exercise of power by the elite set in motion a struggle for survival which, because of the rallying voice of prophecy, ended in revolution. The background of the struggle, however, had its roots in the institution of kingship itself.

In their initial form, Israel's socio-economic structures were relatively egalitarian in that families had approximately equal access to goods and services through a protective extended family and inter-tribal community (Gottwald, 1979: 465). This egalitarianism developed in contrast to the predominant hierarchies of the lowland city-states. The settlements of pre-monarchic Israel were concentrated in less populated areas outside the control of the city-state kings, and were developed in response to the challenges of a frontier (Chaney: 49-50). David's kingship and military unification of the North and South overcame the city-states that still existed in Palestine, bringing them firmly under Israelite control for the first time. They were annexed bodily into Israel, the upper classes and population surrounding them becoming subjects of the crown (Bright: 197).

However, the independent nature of northern Israel was not eliminated even when it was unified with the South under David. In his final years elements of rebellion and movements toward separation gained in strength. Solomon afflicted the North even more, particularly as he restructured it into administrative districts and levied heavy taxation. His governance style pressured the traditional Yahwistic egalitarian orientation, uprooting tribal ties and patterns and reforming Israelite society into a more typical advanced agrarian stratification model. At Solomon's death the northern sector of the "United Kingdom" looked to his son Rehoboam in the hope that the trend would be reversed. Rehoboam's mistake in deciding to listen to his peers (see 1 Kgs 12) was the point at which Jeroboam's prophetically backed leadership emerged and the North rebelled (Bright: 217–227). Using their own ancient style of people-based ratification, the northern assembly called Jeroboam as king to lead them in their bid for a release of pressures (Alt: 246).

The approximately 50 years between Jeroboam and Omri were characterized by a political and religious decentralization in the North. But with Omri's power bid and final establishment on the throne, he was able to set a direction for Israel's development that continued until the Jehu revolution. Omri followed policies in political, socio-economic, and religious areas that paralleled Solomon's by increasing an administrative organization that was grounded in the old city-state models. This brought to the fore the continuing problem of the relationship between "Israelites" and "Canaanites."

The tensions between "Israelite" and "Canaanite" went back to the time of the Judges and early monarchy. The differences were fundamental, between opposite socio-economic and value systems with their corresponding religious orientations. Within a typical centralized agrarian society, the main economic base is the land, organized through land tenure systems that are mostly controlled by urban land holders and worked by the peasantry. Urban economy depends upon the rural economy through its ability to produce a surplus that can support the urban population. "In many respects the economy of the typical agrarian society resembled a tree with roots spreading in every direction, constantly drawing in new resources" (Lenski and Lenski: 184). The system is one-sided; the flow of goods is away from the peasants. Trade occurs internationally between urban centers, dealing mainly with strategic military goods and luxury items. Within this kind of a system, the maintenance of order is especially important since so much depends upon the success of each harvest, and each harvest depends upon months of effort. Disruption of the cycle at any point spells disaster for all parts of the system.

Urban land holders in a centralized state system control the land in a mixture of patrimonial and prebendal land tenure systems. Patrimonial domain is exercised when the land is placed in the hands of a retainer who then inherits the right to that land as a member of a kinship group or lineage. Rights to the land can be pyramided with the peasant always at the base of such an organizational structure, sustaining it by his labor.

Under prebendal domain the land itself is not inherited, but takes the form of a grant to a retainer, who draws income from land that is worked by the peasants who are servants of the state. The grants of income, or prebends, are given in return for the exercise of a particular office. There is always pressure from the landed gentry to move prebendal domain into patrimonial, since the use of prebendal domain implies a greater degree of centralization in contrast to a greater autonomy on the part of the patrimonial domain holders (Wolf: 50–51).

These two typical agrarian land tenure systems contrast with the more diffuse and egalitarian system developed by Israelite villages in the early days of Israel's existence. Their traditional land tenure took the form of a land allotment system based on the premise that Yahweh was the owner of the land and that families inherited the right to partake in the allotment. The arable land, surveyed into economically equal portions, was allotted to families who had the right to its production. Patrimonial inheritance of the allotment kept the land and its produce within families. However, a family did not own its land and could not sell it (see Lev 25:23).

During the pre-monarchic period, these plots of land in the highlands were used for cereal production instead of the better suited vine, olive, or nuts. By the time of the United Monarchy with the grain producing land having come under Israel's control, the terraced hill country could be brought into its more appropriate production (Stager: 11–13). With the Omrids came renewed economic pressure for production on the peasantry, and the traditional tenure system was not strong enough to resist the push to gain more real estate for the landed gentry. Thus the grain producing valleys in the north around the city–states continued under patrimonial and prebendal domain while other land was being bought up, often by the king, forcing small land-owners and peasants off their land. In this way, the crown's land acquisition and orientation to the city clashed with the traditional village value systems.

Lenski's graphic summary of the "typical" agrarian society is appropriate for examining social stratification during the time of the Omrid dynasty. Making clear that the classes in an agrarian society were not merely a series of layers superimposed on one another, the following diagram indicates that there was a "continuum of power and privilege" and not distinct strata.

Figure A = Lenski diagram

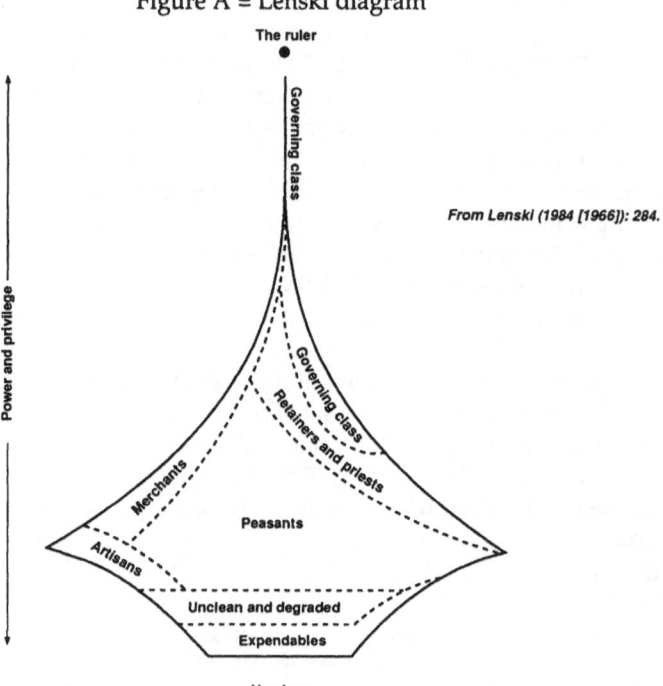

From Lenski (1984 [1966]): 284.

"Although the form of domain as such is relevant to the way a peasant ecosystem is organized, providing the pattern for social relations, it is the way the pattern is utilized by the power–holders which is decisive in shaping the profile of the total system" (Wolf: 56). During the Omrid dynasty, the governing class that controlled the land dominated the peasantry through a system of rent capitalism. Such a process meant that monetary values were assigned to the various factors of production—such as paying to get water, tools, and work animals—and the pressured peasant may have had to borrow money and pay interest on it to maintain land prodution (Wolf: 55). When pressures became overwhelming, the peasant was forced off the land. "At the bottom of the class system in every agrarian society except perhaps for brief periods following great disasters, there was a fairly large class of expendable persons for whom the other members of society had little or no need" (Lenski: 281). During the rule of Ahab and Joram in particular, people who had no control over their downward mobility were pushed into this class. Gottwald and Chaney (in a 1979 lecture) have identified several factors that increase pressure on land tenure systems, and peasant classes in general, that are relevant in this situation.

First, drought and famine were present during this period. Elijah announced the great drought in 1 Kgs 17:1, which lasted three years and about which there is independent evidence from Josephus. Josephus quotes Menander, setting the drought in the time of "Achab" when Ithobalos was king of Tyre (*Jewish Antiquities,* VIII: line 324) The famine that resulted from the drought (1 Kgs 18:2–6) was severe. The drought caused concern in the royal household because it affected the water needs of the royal chariot corps to the extent that even the king and his vizier went to search for new sources (see 1 Kgs 18:5–6). In the Elisha material, too, there is indication of famine. In 2 Kgs 4:38–41 the "sons of the prophets" resorted to strange food to supplement their diet with near disastrous results. During a time of drought and famine, marginal peasants would have been forced off land that could no longer sustain their subsistence needs.

Second, warfare, corvée, and heavy taxes drew men from the land, increasing the load on the family left behind. Taxation would have been used to levy the necessary commodities for tribute, for grain to support the army (both animals and men), and for the building efforts specifically in Samaria, Megiddo, and Hazor.

Third, the marginal land-owners already under pressure would have been vulnerable to being bought out by city entrepreneurs, who would then have had only a single stranded relationship to the land—squeezing from it as much production as possible. Crown land acquisition would have increased latifundialization whereby the previous landed peasant would have become a landless day-laborer. The land-owners would then have moved to change mixed agriculture into agriculture more appropriate to the requirements of the land itself, and so would have decreased the ability of the peasant to live off the land. This, then, would have increased the flight of people into cities where they formed a class of unskilled laborers on the fringes of the society. These factors promoted the shift in balance of wealth from the country into the city, where mercantile and commercial interests predominated.

Fourth, this process increased the incidence of interest-bearing loans which then led into debt-slavery. Foreclosure on loans abetted the transfer of land from the more egalitarian inheritance system into the prebendal and patrimonial land tenure systems, which decreased peasant interest in production, which then led toward lower productivity. The emphasis in Israelite customary law against interest-bearing loans indicates a prohibition against precisely what was taking place in the society.

Therefore, the years covered by the Elijah-Elisha stories were a time of peasant dislocation by pressures from the prevailing royal-urban complex exacerbated by drought and resulting famine. The Elisha stories in particular indicate that the "expendables" gathered into groups called *běnê hannĕbîʾîm*, "sons of the prophets," with Elisha as their leader and protector. The "sons of the prophets" sought both sustenance and refuge, and the Elisha miracle stories focus on the practical concerns of a marginal community for food, shelter, tools, and healing.

In addition to the "expendables" Elisha had contacts within the upper classes of Israelite society, where there was a growing dissatisfaction with the ruling "house of Ahab." The Naboth incident in 1 Kgs 21 and several places in the Elisha legends show the prophet in touch with wealthy people. With Naboth, the story revolves around crown land acquisition vs. the right of Israelite inheritance. False evidence was given against Naboth to the "elders (*hazzĕqēnîm*) and the nobles (*haḥōrîm*) who ruled (*yāšab*) with Naboth in the city" (v. 8). The "elders" and the "nobles" would have been the heads of families who formed a ruling council within the villages (de Vaux: 69). As Gottwald has shown, *yāšab* was an early specialized term for those who exercised political or judgmental authority (1979: 512–34). Thus, Naboth was one of the land holders that formed the upper class in Jezreel.

The Naboth story considered Naboth as an example to the entire class that their "inheritance" of the right to the produce of the land was in jeopardy because of the king's/Jezebel's actions. Their actions followed a style of leadership that did not understand or acknowledge the traditional Israelite rights of inheritance. In the story Ahab understood those rights and seemed to be caught in the middle of a difficult situation between two different land ownership systems. Ahab's solution was to allow Jezebel to exercise her power, and Naboth was put to death on false testimony. If this could happen to Naboth, then the other Israelite land-owners could clearly see their own danger.

Two other examples of the upper classes' role in the growing dissatisfaction with the "house of Ahab" involve people who listened to and supported Elisha. In 2 Kgs 4:42 an unnamed man from Baal-shalishah brought the community gifts of food, indicating his support of the "sons of the prophets" from one who had a surplus. 2 Kings 6:32 relates: "Elisha was sitting in his house and the elders were sitting with him." These are both indications that the upper classes listened to and supported Elisha and his groups, and were probably both angered and frightened by the Naboth incident.

A second, and relatively unexplored area of dissatisfaction is indicated by the story in 2 Kgs 4 of the Shunammite woman (Chaney, personal communication). As she is called an *ʾiššâ gĕdôlâ* and by the indications of her wealth, she is an example of status inconsistency. People who have attained a certain status or rank have a natural tendency to think of themselves in terms of that status or rank and to expect others to do the same. Meanwhile, others have a vested interest in treating people in terms of the lowest possible status or rank (Lenski: 87). The queen, Jezebel, brought an entourage with her who set the prevailing fashion for upper class women in society. However, even if an Israelite woman had the status or rank to match Jezebel's entourage, because of her Israelite birth she would have remained an outsider and lived with inconsistent status—wealth but no power. "This is important for a general theory of stratification if such experiences led individuals to react against the existing social order and the political system which undergirds it" (Lenski: 87). Elisha has the Shunammite woman's allegiance, if not her financial backing, perhaps even to support a revolution that would increase her power to the equivalent of her rank.

In addition to these socio-economic factors, which were increasing the stresses of the assymmetrical structural relationships within Israelite society, there was a growing syncretism within the religious sphere where Yahweh and Baal worship were no longer distinct (Cross: 191f.). As "Yahweh" or "Baal" stood for more than a god to worship, but also represented a social system in which to live, the pressure to choose between them became critical. The Yahweh party retained the traditional values represented in pre-monarchial Israel of an egalitarian societal configuration where Yahweh owned the land and the people were in equal relationship to their god and to each other. The Baal party, on the other hand, fostered the traditional city-state configuration where the gods legitimated the hierarchical structure of king, ruling elite, and a highly developed social stratification. Thus, the question became not merely which god to serve, but in which social configuration to live. Elijah became the spokesman for the re-emphasis of the sacral legitimation of an anti-status, anti-elitist society. He called the king and the people to choose Yahweh over Baal, and thus to reaffirm their commitment to a more egalitarian social structure.

In addition to the pressures to reverse a hierarchical kingship style, there were growing indications that the kings of the "house of Ahab" had lost Yahweh's commission or blessing. The anointing ritual from the time of Saul and David had included the idea that the king was anointed because he was endowed with the divine blessing (bĕrākâ) and thus set apart (Gray: 92). In the North this concept persisted in the belief that a king could only be a true ruler when he evidenced his possession of the blessing by some natural ability or aptitude. The converse was true—that the anointing of a prince simply because he was the son of the king abused the rite. Thus Joram's lack of success and Jehu's popularity indicated the blessing was Jehu's, confirmed and amplified by the rite of anointing (Gray: 540). Joram caught the tail end of the difficulties begun by his father Ahab; and although he tried to ease matters by removing some of the more objectionable Baal cult objects, while Jezebel still had power, his hands were tied. "Real reform was impossible, even had Jehoram desired it, as long as the sinister shadow of the queen-mother fell over the land" (Bright: 244). Therefore, with socio-economic pressures upon the land and the people, with the Yahweh party growing in subversive strength, with the suitability of Ahab's dynasty to uphold Yahweh worship faithfully and social praxis in growing doubt, the result was a particularly bloody revolution (Gottwald: 1976).

After the revolution, oral stories of the prophets' words and actions were gathered together to provide a written account legitimating Jehu. The Elijah-Elisha cycle accomplished a dual objective: first, it showed by the commission at Mt. Horeb that Yahweh had designated that the "house of Ahab" should be overthrown by means of his prophets; second, it showed that Jezebel's foreign influence in the spheres of both politics and religion was to be emphatically destroyed by the pro-Yahweh party through Jehu. "From the designation by Yahweh, and the acclamation of the people, to the extermination of the fallen royal house that had preceded him, everything that took place, as far as the kingdom of Israel was concerned (2 Kgs 9), was basically the same as had been experienced by their ancestors from the time of Saul to that of Omri" (Alt: 250). Charismatic kingship needed prophetic designation, popular acclaim, or both. Thus Elisha, fulfilling Elijah's commission on Mt. Horeb, designated Jehu as the next king over Israel.

2. 1 Kings 17–19: Literary Analysis

The set of stories in 1 Kgs 17–19 presents a composite picture of Elijah the prophet and his actions. First, Elijah stands as the authentic mediator of the divine word; then in his role as mediator, he forces a choice between Yahweh or Baal; and finally, after a Moses-like theophany, he returns to call Elisha as his successor. Although the three chapters now form one entity, they are made up of smaller units that can be explored by structural analysis. The compiler has used material of differing types, assembling the stories along the lines of a carefully formed plan. The mosaic-like effect of the units betrays the presence and use of already existing material (Campbell: 142ff.). The presentation of the stories flows from the initial pronouncement of the drought and resulting famine to Elijah's calling a successor who feeds the people. In between these outer limits, the matrix of the narrative is Yahweh vs. Baal, investigated through such questions as who controls the weather, rain, and dew; who answers a prophetic summons; who feeds prophets and people; and whose is the theophanic voice? The repetitions of Hebrew words and phrases in the stories and the resulting structures guide the reader/hearer to the focus of each unit. Therefore, paying attention to the structures of the individual units in chapters 17-19 will inform the presentation of Elijah's prophetic role in proclaiming Yahweh, not Baal, to be the God of Israel.

Chapter 17

Chapter 17 presents Elijah as an authentic mediator of the divine word. The pronouncement in v. 1 and the conclusion in v. 24 form an inclusio. Elijah claims that the end of the drought will be "by his word," and the confession of the woman is that the prophet's word has proven to be true.

> v. 1 As the Lord, the God of Israel lives, before whom I stand, there shall be no dew or rain these years except by the command of my word.

> v. 24 And the woman said to Elijah, "Now this I know, that a man of God are you and the word of Yahweh is truly in your mouth."

Elijah's role as mediator means that he acts as the intermediary or medium in effecting actions. In his prophetic role he stands before Yahweh, perhaps observing the divine council as does Micaiah in 1 Kgs 22:19f., behaving as a prophetic courier of the divine word (Cross: 187). "Form-critical analysis of the prophetic forms of speech has yielded the information that the prophet's office is that of messenger and that the fundamental message he brings is the judgment" (Cross: 189). Elijah's prophetic message is that Ahab has been praying to the wrong weather god, and the judgment is the drought, pronounced by the courier until his word proclaims otherwise. In between the pronouncement and the validation (vv. 1 and 24), the rest of chapter 17 functions to exemplify the authority of the prophet and the reliability of his word. The concluding confession of the widow in v. 24 is the first step in the community's acceptance of that authority and reliability.

The structure of this chapter contains three parts or scenes. Scene 1 (vv. 2–7) uses repetition to form a simple movement from command to response.

COMMAND:	RESPONSE:
the word of Yahweh says	and he went and did according to the word of Yahweh
COMMAND:	RESPONSE:
go, turn eastward and hide in the wadi Kerith which is before the Jordan	he dwelt in the wadi Kerith which is before the Jordan
drink from the wadi food from ravens	ravens brought food from the wadi he drank

The first repetition is *dābār*, "word," for just as the "word" of the prophet is spoken pronouncing the drought, the "word" of Yahweh sends the prophet into a protected place to hide. The word of Yahweh commands that the prophet drink from the wadi and be provided with food, and in the repetition the command is accomplished. Thus, by the command-response structure, the word of Yahweh has sent the prophet into hiding and has provided him with sustenance.

The complication that moves the action into scene 2 is that the wadi dries up, and the prophet is caught as a victim of his own pronouncement. Scene 2 (vv. 8–16) continues the same command-response structure but contains an extra complication in the middle. No longer do simple agents directly responsive to the word of Yahweh provide the prophet with food, but now Yahweh has commanded that food be produced by a person who is herself having trouble. In order to make a bread-cake for Elijah, Yahweh must provide the flour and oil. Although the prophet begins passively to receive food in scene 1, here he must actively intercede to provide food for himself and the widow's household.

COMMAND:	RESPONSE:
the word of Yahweh says:	
arise, go to Zarephath and dwell there	he arose and went to Zarephath and he came to the gate of the city
food from a widow woman	request for food from the widow

COMPLICATION: the widow has nothing except a handful of meal and a little oil; she and her son are facing death

COMMAND:	RESPONSE:
come, do according to your word	and she went and did according to the word of Elijah
make me a bread-cake and bring it to me first	and she ate, she and he and her household for days

For thus says Yahweh, God of Israel:
| the jar of flour shall not end | the jar of flour did not end |
| the juglet of oil shall not diminish | the juglet of oil did not diminish |

CONCLUSION: according to the word of Yahweh which he spoke through Elijah

Repetitions of *dābār*, and now repetitions of the verb *kilkēl* (to provide with food), direct the actions in both scenes. The prophet pronounces the "word" but is caught by the result of its power when the wadi dries up. He must then become a mediator of the "word" in order to provide life for individuals. No longer does food come from Yahweh's word alone, for now the prophet has become part of the process of producing food.

Thus, scenes 1 and 2 are closely bound together both by the similarity in their structures, and by repetitive patterns:

Scene 1:2
wayhî dĕbar yhwh ʾēlāyw lēʾmōr

Scene 1:4
ṣiwwîtî lĕkalkelkā šām

Scene 2:8
wayhî dĕbar yhwh ʾēlāyw lēʾmōr

Scene 2:9
ṣiwwîtî lĕkalkelkā šām

Scene 1:2
wayhî dĕbar yhwh
5
wayyaʿaś kidbar yhwh

Scene 2:8
wayhî dĕbar yhwh
13
ʿăśî kidbārēk
15
wattaʿăśeh kidbar ʾēlîyāhû
16
kidbar yhwh ʾăšer dibber bĕyad ʾēlîyāhû

The sequence of the "word of Yahweh" is finalized in v. 24 with the widow's confession: "the word of Yahweh is truly in your mouth"— *ûdĕbar yhwh bĕpîkā ʾĕmet*.

Scene 3 (vv. 17–24) differs in style from the preceding scenes for it is arranged in a chiastic structure. The change in style illustrates for the first time that these chapters are a compilation of independent Elijah narratives. The story in scene 3 centers upon an issue that is not of major importance in the Elijah cycle of chapters 17–19. In a chiastic structure, the center of the chiasm contains the emphasis, and here the center focuses upon "the widow, the fatherless, and the sojourner," three groups of people who are particularly helpless and stand under the special protection of Yahweh. The complaints of the widow to Elijah, and Elijah to Yahweh, are parallel and address the question of prophetic intent:

> woman to Elijah (v. 18): "Why are you interfering in my affairs, man of God? Did you come to me to bring to remembrance my iniquity and to kill my son?"
>
> Elijah to Yahweh (v. 20): "Have you even brought evil upon the **widow** with whom I am **sojourning** to kill her **son**?"

The structure of this short story reinforces the prophet's actions in resuscitating the widow's son:

18	ʾîš hāʾĕlōhîm ... lĕhāmît ʾet bĕnî
19	ʾāmar nātan lāqaḥ ʿālâ
20	wayyiqrāʾ ʾel yhwh wayōʾmār yhwh ʾĕlōhay ... lĕhāmît ʾet bĕnāh
21–22	wayyiqrāʾ ʾel yhwh wayyōʾmār yhwh ʾĕlōhay ... wayĕḥî
23	lāqaḥ yārad nātan ʾāmar
23–24	ḥay bĕnek ... ʾîš ʾĕlōhîm

18	Man of God ... to kill my son
19	said give took went up
20	he called to Yahweh and said, O Yahweh, my God ... to kill her son
22	he called to Yahweh and said, O Yahweh, my God ... and he lived
23	took went down gave said
23-24	your son lives ... Man of God

Although the structure of scene 3 intends to draw attention to Yahweh's protection and life-giving to the widow, fatherless, and sojourner, the Elijah cycle uses the story for a different purpose: Elijah's mediation efforts save the boy. The second time Elijah calls out to Yahweh, he names the intended effect that his sympathetic magic is to produce: "return, please, the life (*nepeš*) of this lad to his middle" (v. 21). Yahweh hears the voice of Elijah, pays attention to his request, returns the *nepeš* to the boy, and the boy lives. Thus Elijah demonstrates effective prophetic mediation.

The mother's confession while concluding this scene frames the chapter, and finalizes the movement within ch. 17. After pronouncing the drought, Elijah is sent to hide in a wadi where food is provided without his intervention. Elijah is next sent to Zarephath, a town in Phoenicia between Tyre and Sidon, where the prophet must intervene with mediation in order that food be provided. Finally, Elijah is called upon to intervene in a situation that is even more difficult—the apparent death of the widow's son. Each scene in ch. 17 moves Elijah's authority one step further. First, he responds to Yahweh's word; second, he participates in Yahweh's promise that food will be provided; third, the prophet initiates, and Yahweh responds, to his request. Finally, the confession of the widow indicates her acceptance of that authority, and if a Phoenician woman can accept it, then all the more is the community expected to accept the reliability of the prophet's mediation of Yahweh's word.

Chapter 18

Chapter 18 presents Elijah in his role as mediator forcing a choice for Yahweh or Baal. Chapter 18 begins, after a time of transition, with the word of Yahweh commanding Elijah to reappear from hiding: "Go, appear to Ahab that I may give rain upon the face of the earth" (v. 1). Again the initial pronouncement and the final action (the rain) frame the chapter. The first scene explores the situation at court into which Elijah has been commanded to appear. The second scene dramatizes the confrontation between Yahweh and Baal, for the result of Elijah's appearance is the necessity for the people to make a choice. The third scene is the culmination of the command for Elijah's appearance and the people's decision for Yahweh, as at last the rains come.

The scenes also show a movement in location that may reflect the larger purpose of the Elijah cycle—from Samaria to Mt. Carmel to Jezreel. The importance of Jezreel as an Israelite center in contrast to Samaria's Baalistic orientation will be examined later in the discussion on 1 Kgs 21 and 2 Kgs 9. In ch. 18, however, scene changes help to underscore the theme that is developed further on in the cycle. Before Elijah appears Ahab is in Samaria, where the drought/famine is severe. After the central scene, in which people must choose between Yahweh and Baal, Ahab rides to Jezreel, replete and in the rain. Within the context of Yahweh vs. Baal, after the people have made their decision for Yahweh, Ahab changes his residence, indicating his acquiescence in the people's affirmation.

Scene 1 (vv. 2–15) introduces the royal household and gives some details about the situation into which Elijah is appearing. The limits of the scene are indicated by the oaths that form a pattern including 1 Kgs 17:1:

> 17:1 As Yahweh the God of Israel lives, **before whom I stand**, there shall be these years neither dew nor rain (*maṭār*) except by my word.
>
> 18:1 And after many days, the word of Yahweh came to Elijah in the third year saying: "Go, make your appearance to Ahab, that I may give rain (*maṭār*) upon the face of the earth."
>
> 18:15 And Elijah said: "As Yahweh Seba'oth lives, **before whom I stand**, today I will appear to [Ahab]."

The pronouncement in 17:1 is of the drought, and this scene gives an indication of the effects of that drought in two parts, each indicated by an internal repetition. The first part (vv. 3–6) has two elements connected by the repetition of the verb *kārat*, "cut off," in the *Hiphil*. The second part (v. 14) is divided by the triple repetition of the phrase: "Go, say to my lord, here is Elijah!" Verses 4 and 13 contain almost identical repetitions, which form an inclusio that ties the two parts together.

4   And it was when Jezebel destroyed (*kārat*) the prophets of
    Yahweh, Obadiah took a hundred prophets and hid them, fifty
    men (each) in the cave, and **provided them with food and
    water**.

13 Has it not been reported to my lord what I did when Jezebel
    killed (*hārag*) the prophets of Yahweh? And I hid from the
    prophets a hundred men, fifty by fifty men, in the cave and I
    provided them food and water?

4   *wayĕhî bĕhakĕrît ʾîzebel*   13 *bahărōg ʾîzebel*
    ʾet nĕbîʾê yhwh   *ʾet nĕbîʾê yhwh*
    ʾōbadyāhû mēʾâ nĕbîʾîm wayyahbîʾēm   *wāʾahbiʾ minnĕbîʾe yhwh mēʾa ʾîš*
    ḥămišîm ʾîš   *ḥămišîm ḥămišîm ʾîš*
    bammĕʿārâ wĕkilkĕlām leḥem wāmāyim   *bammĕʿārâ waʾăkalkĕlēm leḥem wāmāyim*

The descriptions in these verses differ in only one significant aspect.
Jezebel "destroys" in v. 4 (*hikrît*), while in v. 13 she "kills" (*hārag*) the
prophets. The use of the more common verb "to kill" in v. 13 draws
attention to the use of "destroy" in v. 4 and its repetition in v. 5.

4   And it was when Jezebel **destroyed** the prophets of Yahweh,
    Obadiah took a hundred prophets and hid them, fifty men
    (each) in the cave and provided them with food and water.

5   And Ahab said to Obadiah, "Go in the land to all the springs
    of water and to all the wadis; perhaps we may find grass and
    we will keep alive horse and mule, and will not **destroy** from
    the animals.

During the drought and the time of Elijah's disappearance, the famine
has become severe in Samaria. The main characters in this scene are
Ahab, Jezebel, and Obadiah. Ahab's concern is the effect of the drought
on his military equipment: the horses for chariots and mules for the supply train. Jezebel's concern is the elimination of the prophets of Yahweh
from Samaria. Obadiah's concern is to hold back death, for the prophets
and possibly for the animals. As Obadiah provides the prophets with
food and water, the same verb *kilkēl* is used as in 17:4 and 9 where
Yahweh commanded that food be provided to the prophet, Elijah,
through the ravens and the widow in Zarephath. Each of the four times
when *kilkēl* is used, an agent of Yahweh provides life for a prophet(s) of
Yahweh in the face of death. Again, as in ch. 17, the theme of hiding is
coupled with the threat of death—a death that is turned around by the
provision of food through Yahweh's agent. Thus, Yahweh's command to
the prophet Elijah is: "Go, appear to Ahab"—appear in a situation where

death threatens prophets through Jezebel, Ahab's wife, and life continues only by hiding.

Verses 6–7 supply the transition between the two parts of scene 1. One of the functions of scene 1 is to retard the action, building tension before Elijah's actual appearance to Ahab. The vizier would normally accompany the king, but here the narrative emphasizes Obadiah's aloneness:

> They divided the land for themselves to pass through it; Ahab went on one path by himself, and Obadiah went on another path by himself.

Humor and pathos are present in the meeting between Obadiah and Elijah as Obadiah may indeed have wished that he had kept to traditional policy and accompanied the king. Although he is deferential to Elijah, he is not overjoyed at his role of courier; dealings with this prophet are uncertain at best.

> When Obadiah was on the path, look at this! Elijah is coming to meet him! And he recognized him, and he fell on his face and he said, "Is it really you, my lord, Elijah?"
>
> And he said to him, "It is I. Go, say to your lord, 'Here is Elijah!'"
>
> But he said, "What, have I sinned? For you are giving your servant into the hand of Ahab to kill me!"

This second part of scene 1 is balanced with the triple repetition of "Go, say to your lord, 'Here is Elijah!'" (vv. 8, 11, 14) and Obadiah's response that this action will result in his death. During the years of the drought, Ahab has been seeking Elijah throughout the surrounding kingdoms, but without success. Now Obadiah is afraid that once he leaves Elijah the "spirit of Yahweh" will lift him up to an unknown place. Both of these sections call to mind 2 Kgs 2 where the "sons of the prophets" pressure Elisha into allowing them to seek out Elijah "lest the spirit of Yahweh has lifted him up" (v. 16) into the surrounding hills, and they, too, have no success in finding him. Just as neither Ahab's nor the "sons of the prophets'" seeking could find Elijah, Yahweh's word alone causes him to appear. Until Obadiah hears that word, he protests his commission. Thus, this part of scene 1 concludes with Elijah's repetition of the formula used in 17:1—oath, identification of his role, message:

> As Yahweh Seba'oth lives, before whom I stand, today I will appear to him.

The authority of the prophet stands firm. Obadiah as a fearer of Yahweh must play his role as courier—no longer hiding the prophets from death, but announcing the appearance of the prophet for life.

Scene 2 (vv. 16-40) presents the call to the people to make their own decision for life or death as Elijah forces the issue over which god they will follow, Yahweh or Baal. This scene is the centerpiece in chapters 17–19, and brings forth the essential decision that was Elijah's emphasis. Although the entire cycle has been used to legitimate Jehu's revolution, in this scene the underlying religious question is settled, in the same kind of way that the question/answer is brought forth at the end of Joshua. Just as adherence to Yahweh and his commandments formulates the egalitarian style of charismatic leadership, so adherence to the Baals places in the forefront the Canaanite stratified style. The people and their leaders can no longer go limping along on two opinions; they must choose between them. When Elijah does appear before Ahab, he is attacked: "Is this you, troubler of Israel?" (v. 17). Elijah's answer is an accusation against Ahab and his leadership: "I have not troubled Israel, but you and the house of your fathers when you forsook the commandments of Yahweh and went after the Baals" (v. 18). Now the accusation is clear, for not only has Ahab focused on the wrong weather god, he has also put Israel under cultic jeopardy by the admission of the Baals into the ruling structure.

Although this scene is the longest narrative in chs. 17–19 and has the most pieces of action and instruction, its basic structure is a simple chiasm formed by the repetition of the verb ʿānâ, "to answer." Complementary repetitions of the verbs pāsaḥ, "to limp," nāgaš, "to draw near," and qārāʾ, "to call," serve to emphasize particular parts of the narrative, with the nouns qôl, "voice," and dābār, "word," appearing at crucial junctures. In contrast to a linear reading, where the climax comes with the fire falling to consume Elijah's offering, in a chiastic structure the important section is the middle of the chiasm, vv. 25-29. The cluster of repetitions as well as the triple use of ʿānâ establishes the significance of these verses. Elijah plays the role of mediator between the people and Yahweh as he issues the challenge and organizes the confrontation.

Figure B: The Structure of 1Kgs 18:21–38

Basic Structure

Verses				
21	22–24	25–29	30–37	38
		ʿanāh		
		ʾên ʿanāh		
		ʾên ʿanāh		
	ʿanāh		ʿanāh	
	ʿanāh		ʿanāh	
lōʾ ʿanāh				the answer of fire

Auxiliary Repetitions

Verses				
21	22–24	25–29	30–37	38
pāsaḥ		pāsaḥ		
nāgaš			nāgaš	
			nāgaš	
dābār	dābār		dābār	
			dābār	
			dābār	

Verses:	22–24	25–29
	qěrāʾtem běšēm ʾělōhêkem	qirʾû běšēm ʾělōhêkem
	ʾeqrāʾ běšēm yhwh	wayyiqrěʾû běšēm habbaʿal
		ʾên qôl
		qirʾû běqôl gādôl
		wayyiqrěʾû běqôl gādôl
		ʾên qôl

Within the five sections of this scene, the chiastic structure balances the movement from "no answer" in v. 21 to the "answer" of fire in v. 38 and the response of the people in v. 39. In v. 21 Elijah challenges the people: "How long will you go limping upon two opinions?" But the people do not yet answer Elijah "a word." As in scene 3 of ch. 17, the prophet names the desired response: both times Yahweh listens to the voice of his prophet, and in v. 38 Yahweh answers Elijah with fire. Again, the authority of Elijah has proved reliable, and as the confession of the widow was the response in ch. 17, so now the people respond, choosing Yahweh as their God.

The second set in the chiasm has Elijah being the instructor. First, in vv. 22–24 he instructs the prophets of Baal to prepare their bull, calling upon the name of Baal to answer with fire. In these verses, the people do answer, acquiescing to the contest rules with "good is the word" (v. 24). In the balancing verses Elijah involves the people in the preparation of the altar for the Yahweh sacrifice, drawing upon the symbols of their historical connection with Yahweh: twelve stones for the altar according to the number of the sons of Jacob; the reminder that the word of Yahweh caused these twelve to be called by the name of Israel; twelve jars of water poured into the trench (Carlson 1969: 424). Finally, Elijah declares his mediator status and demands that Yahweh answer:

> Yahweh, God of Abraham Isaac and Israel, today let it be
> known that you are God in Israel and I am your servant, and
> (that) by your word I have done all these things. Answer me,
> O Yahweh, answer me!

The center of the conflict contains the non-response of Baal, which is the point of the contest. Just as Baal cannot control the rain/drought, neither can Baal answer the request of his prophets. Elijah instructs the prophets to prepare the bull according to their own ceremonies; Elijah taunts the prophets, moving them to even greater fervor; but the prophets of Baal cannot raise a response from their god. The action is centered around the use of the verbs $qārā^{\jmath}$ and $\text{^{c}}ānâ$ with Elijah instructing and the prophets of Baal responding:

> Call upon the name of your god...
>   and they called upon the name of Baal...
>   O Baal, answer us!
>   But there was no voice and no answer.
> And they limped around the altar...
>   Call in a loud voice...
>   and they called in a loud voice...
>   they cut themselves until the blood ran...
>   But there was no voice and no answer and no attentiveness.

The prophets of Baal have had their turn with frenzy, blood and frustration. Baal has been proven ineffective, and the people affirm that Yahweh, he is their God! The choice is finally made. Those who were led astray by the leadership of Ahab have been confronted by the necessity to decide, for they can no longer limp along but must make their own choice for death or life. The people made the choice for life, the prophets of Baal for death—and death follows swiftly.

The people's choice for life results in the life-giving rain of scene 3. Here is the culmination of Elijah's claim in 17:1, that neither dew nor rain shall happen except by his word. He has spoken the word in scene 2, Yahweh has listened to his request for an answer, and in scene 3 the rains come. Scene 3 (vv. 41-46) is organized around the seven-fold repetition of the verb ʿālâ, "to go up," with the pivotal center being when the young lad is instructed to return seven times to look for the rain which comes on the seventh.

v. 41	Elijah said to Ahab, "Go up"	ʿălē
42	Ahab **went up**...and Elijah **went up** to the top of Mt. Carmel	wayyaʿăle wĕʾēliyāhû ʿalâ
43	Elijah said to his helper, "Go up please"...and he **went up**	ʿălē naʾ wayyaʿal
44	a cloud **coming up** from the sea... and Elijah said, "**Go up**"	ʿōlâ ʿălē

In addition to this repetition of ʿālâ, gešem, one of the words for rain, is repeated three times. The word gešem was also used in 17:7 and 14:

v. 7 and it happened sometime later the wadi dried up, for rain (gešem) did not happen in the land.

v. 14 For thus says Yahweh, the God of Israel, "The jar of meal shall not come to an end and the juglet of oil shall not diminish until the day Yahweh gives rain (gešem) upon the face of the earth."

In contrast, māṭār was used for rain in 17:1 and 18:1, both introductory pronouncements.

Scene 3 establishes one more victory for Yahweh over Baal by displaying that Yahweh and not Baal "brings the fructifying rain which makes the desert bloom" (Cross: 151). In ch. 18, Elijah has appeared to Ahab, the people have made their choice, and now the rain to end the drought presents the hope that Yahweh's victory will have permanent consequences upon the leadership style of the king in Israel. Just as the holocaust offering (ʿōlôt) was presented and accepted in scene 2, the actions of Ahab, Elijah, and his helper in "going up" correspond to the "coming up" of the rain cloud from the sea. And both Ahab and Elijah precede the rain to Jezreel, the Israelite center of government in the North.

Chapter 19

Chapter 19 presents Elijah in another aspect of his mediative role, as a prophet who stands in the tradition of Moses. It begins with Jezebel's reaction to the slaughter of the prophets of Baal, but unlike the pattern in the preceding chapters, her curse is not fulfilled in the final scene. Instead Elijah calls his successor, an event which proves Jezebel's curse was as impotent as were her prophets in ch. 18. In the first scene, however, the prophet flees from retribution and the threat of death—a death that Elijah requests in his despair. Yet the prophet, being provided with food through an agent of Yahweh, no longer flees but goes on to a theophany. The second scene consummates the confrontation on Mt. Carmel, where Yahweh's answer was fire. To counter the impression that Yahweh's presence was to be identified through the same kind of manifestations as Baal, the theophany clarifies that Yahweh speaks through word and not through physical element; through human beings, not in spite of them. The third scene completes the cycle from famine to food as the prophet gains a helper who feeds the people, and who ministers to him as Joshua did to Moses. Chapter 19 ties Elijah firmly to Moses, providing continuity between the theophanic words spoken at Horeb/Sinai.

In scene 1 (vv. 1–8), the threat of Jezebel's persecution pressures Elijah into a crisis where he must decide if he will continue to serve as Yahweh's prophet. The two themes of hiding and feeding are picked up and followed through to their conclusion by the end of the chapter. Elijah hid in the wadi Kerith at Yahweh's command; Obadiah hid the prophets who were in jeopardy from Jezebel's persecution; and now Elijah, facing that same persecution, flees into the wilderness. He even goes to the extent of requesting death, for he sees no hope of continuing to stand against the power of the state. Just as ravens and a widow provided food to Elijah in ch. 17, and Obadiah provided food and drink for the prophets in ch. 18, here another agent, the *mal'ak* ("messenger") of Yahweh, provides food and drink for the prophet in the wilderness. But now Elijah must make a decision. "To be concealed in the cave and preserved with food and water is to remain alive, but not, according to Elijah's own words, to remain a prophet" (Coote: 117).

The first scene in ch. 19 is structured in two parts: around the repetition of the word *nepeš*, "life," in the first half, and around the verb, *'akal*, "to eat" in the second. The scene pivots around the transition phrase *wĕhinnē ze* ("look at this!") in v. 5. Ahab tells his wife Jezebel what Elijah had done, that Elijah had killed the prophets of Baal with the sword, and Jezebel responds with an oath:

> Thus may the gods do (LXX—to me) and more if by (LXX—this) time tomorrow I do not make your life like the life of one from them.

The oath formula that Jezebel uses is a common one, used eleven other times in the literature, although in slightly different form when used by non-Israelites. The two times the oath is used by a non-Israelite (Ben-hadad in 1 Kgs 20:10 and here) two differences appear in the formula. In the ten Israelite uses, with Yahweh the subject twice and Elohim the rest of the time, the verbs *ʿāśâ*, "to do," and *yāsap*, "to increase," are singular. With Ben-hadad and Jezebel the subject is Elohim, but the verbs are plural. The second difference is that in these two places the verbs have the paragogic *nun*, which in Aramaic and Arabic is the regular termination (Kautzsch: 129). The word *nepeš* has no equivalent in English, but covers a range of meanings that include: "living being, life, self, person, desire, appetite, emotion, passion [and perhaps] soul" (Brown, Driver, Briggs: 659). The repetition of *nepeš* begins in Jezebel's oath:

v. 2	I will make your *nepeš*	*napšĕkā*
	like the *nepeš*	*kĕnepeš*
3	and he feared . . . and he went	
	for his *nepeš*	*ʾel napšô*
4	and he asked his *nepeš* to die	*ʾet napšô*
5	enough! take my *nepeš*	*rab . . . qaḥ napšî*

In 17:21, Elijah requested that Yahweh return the *nepeš* of the lad so that he might live, and Yahweh listened and responded to that request. Here, however, Yahweh may hear the prophet's request for death, but instead of taking Elijah's *nepeš*, Yahweh sends a messenger to provide food and water. The food is the same kind of bread-cake the widow made in 17:13, and the water is in a similar juglet to the oil in 17:12, 14, and 16. In the second half of scene 1, the verb *ʾākal*, "to eat," is repeated four times, in a command-response pattern similar to the first two scenes in ch. 17:

Command:	*Response:*
the messenger was touching him and he said to him	
arise, eat!	and he ate and drank and he returned and lay down
the messenger of Yahweh returned a second time and he touched him and he said, arise, eat! for the journey is too	
great (*rab*) for you	and he arose and ate and drank and he went

The reason for the food is given the second time the messenger arouses Elijah, and the repetition of *rab* ties the two parts of the scene together. Yahweh has provided food to keep the prophet alive and to make his journey to Mt. Horeb possible.

Several elements are subtle references to Moses, and indicate the reason for Elijah's journey to Horeb for another theophany. In Exodus 32, Moses returned to Horeb after the slaying within the camp, and Elijah goes to Horeb after the slaying of the prophets of Baal. Although the designation "forty days and nights" may simply indicate a long period of time, nevertheless that same time unit is used throughout the Moses material (see Exod 24:18, 34:28; and Deut 9:9,11,18; 10:10). As Elijah arrives at the mountain he goes into the cave, as Moses hid in a cleft in the presence of Yahweh in Exodus 33.

Scene 2 (vv. 6–18) contains the theophany and the commission. Yahweh's question and Elijah's complaint provide a repetition that forms an inclusio bracketing the theophany and continuing the "Mosaic atmosphere" (Carlson 1969: 432–33). Elijah's complaint against the prevailing power system contains three elements with which any member of the Yahweh party could identify. First, that he has been very jealous/zealous for Yahweh corresponds to the jealous nature of Yahweh stated in Exod 20:5, 34:14; Deut 4:24; 5:9; 6:15. Second, the "sons of Israel," perhaps a general reference to the opposition party, have abandoned Yahweh's covenant, they have thrown down the altars, and they have killed prophets with the sword, thus refusing to abide by the contract with their jealous God. The third part is Elijah's cry that he alone is left, and they seek his *nepeš* to take it, which reflects Jezebel's curse and is a very human cry by anyone standing against the overwhelming pressures of the state.

The intent of the theophany is to exhibit the difference between Yahweh and Baal. "In the earliest poetic sources the language depicting Yahweh as divine warrior manifest is borrowed almost directly from Canaanite descriptions of the theophany of Ba'al as storm god" (Cross: 147). As can be seen in Psalm 29, the Canaanite traditions of the storm god have been "only slightly modified for use in the early cultus of Yahweh" (Cross: 151–56). In Psalm 29, the *qôl*, "voice," of Yahweh is manifested through thunder, striking with fire, making the desert writhe, and breaking the cedars (with wind?). In contrast, because of the alarming syncretism in the ninth century, the climax of this theophany is the silent sound—the *qôl děmāmâ daqqâ* (Coote, 1981: 118). The triple repetition—

v. 11	Yahweh was not in the wind	lō᾽ barûaḥ yhwh
	Yahweh was not in the earthquake	lō᾽ baraʿaš yhwh
v. 12	Yahweh was not in the fire—	lō᾽ baʾēš yhwh

perhaps should each be translated "Yahweh was no longer in the storm" (Cross: 194; Carlson, 1969: 434–35).

Upon hearing this voice of Yahweh, Elijah comes to the entrance of the cave and stands in Yahweh's presence (v. 13) as he was commanded to do in v. 11, and as he had claimed to do in 17:1 and 18:15. Again this indicates a Moses-like intimacy with Yahweh (see Num 12:6–8a). The commission terminates the drama of Yahweh vs. Baal with the promise of an overwhelming victory for the jealous God of Horeb/Sinai (Carlson, 1969: 438). Elijah stands in Yahweh's presence and receives the word of revolution—the commission to overthrow the existing power structures and to anoint a new ruler, Jehu. The commission legitimates the Jehu rebellion and allows Elisha, the inheritor of the spirit of Elijah, to accomplish the mission as a spiritual son of Elijah (Carlson, 1969: 439). The final reassurance is of a remnant who are also standing firm against the pressures so that Elijah, no matter his feelings, does not stand alone.

Scene 3 (vv. 19–21), the final scene of the three chapters, begins the new era. The scene is packed with verbs, and the action moves from Elijah leaving Horeb and finding Elisha, to Elisha leaving the people he has just fed and following Elijah to serve him. The two major repetitions are the number 12 and the preposition ᾽aḥărê, "after." Although Ahab could not "find" Elijah (18:10), Elijah has no trouble "finding" Elisha, who is plowing a field with 12 pair of oxen. Agricultural methodology in the Mediterranean ecotype called for a scratch plow, which as Wolf describes, would certainly not have needed 12 pair of animals.

> Essentially [the scratch plow] is a crooked stick. The cultivator lays hold of one end, the other is shod with metal; the plow is drawn by a pair of draft animals, usually oxen. It is light and easily transported; it is cheap to make and easily repaired (Wolf: 32).

Thus, the repetition here of "12," in the same way as in ch. 18 with the 12's surrounding the rebuilding of the altar, firmly places Elisha in relation to the history and theology of Israel, as the earlier "12" did for Elijah.

After Elijah throws his mantle upon Elisha, passing by in the same manner as Yahweh in the previous scene, Elisha:

v. 20	ran **after** Elijah	*ʾaḥărê ʾēlîyahû*
	"let me go **after** you"	*ʾaḥărêkā*
v. 21	and he returned from **after** him	*mēʾaḥărāw*
	(and he fed the people)	
	and he went **after** Elijah	*ʾaḥărê ʾēlîyahû*

"Elisha follows after Elijah and serves him, replacing the lad whom Elijah left at Beersheba" (v. 3) (Coote, 1981: 120). Thus Elisha's actions in this scene complete both this chapter and the whole unit of chs. 17–19. Elijah's potential death as the last prophet of Yahweh turns into the calling of his successor. Elijah's pronouncement of a drought and famine turns into the feeding of the people with meat. Elijah's authority as a prophet of Yahweh confronted the king and called the people to make a choice. Elisha's authority as a prophet, enhanced by his relationship to Elijah, feeds and ministers to the community.

3. The Elijah/Elisha Cycle as Legitimation Narrative

The second set of Elijah stories, found in 1 Kgs 21, 2 Kgs 1, and 2 Kgs 2:1–18, presents another kind of unified narrative than that found in 1 Kgs 17–19. These stories in the Elijah cycle are used to identify Elisha as Elijah's successor in fulfilling the three-part commission of 1 Kgs 19:15–16.

> And the Lord said to him, "Go, return on your way to the wilderness of Damascus, and when you arrive, you shall anoint Hazael to be king over Syria (see 2 Kgs 8:7–15);
>
> and Jehu the son of Nimshi you shall anoint to be king over Israel (see 2 Kgs 9);
>
> and Elisha the son of Shaphat of Abel-meholah you shall anoint to be prophet in your place" (see 2 Kgs 2:1–18).

In 2 Kgs 2:1–18, Elisha becomes the legitimate inheritor of the spirit of Elijah and thus is the one through whom the rest of the commission is accomplished. In 2 Kings 8:7–15, Elisha, as Elijah before him in 2 Kgs 1, mediates the power of life or death as it relates to a king. In 2 Kgs 9, Elisha completes the commission by anointing Jehu. 2 Kgs 9 and 1 Kgs 21 are connected through the location, Jezreel, and through the references to the property of Naboth the Jezreelite. Isolation of these narratives from the surrounding literature enables us to identify them as one cycle written down for a purpose. Therefore, in this section we will pay attention to the ways in which these Elijah and Elisha stories are tied together carefully and related to each other.

2 Kings 2:1–18

> and Elisha the son of Shaphat of Abel-meholah you shall anoint to be prophet in your place.

In response to the third part of the commission, Elisha becomes the successor to Elijah's authority in 2 Kgs 2:1–18. As was noted in the discussion of 1 Kgs 19, Elijah became identified with Moses. As Elijah was like Moses, so in this chapter is Elisha like Joshua. This identification begins in v. 1 where Elijah and Elisha set out from Gilgal. Although "this Gilgal from which Elijah and Elisha went down (v. 2) to Bethel, cannot have been the Gilgal between Jericho and the Jordan" (Burney: 264), nevertheless "Gilgal" does provide an immediate association with Josh 4:19–24.

> v. 20: And these 12 stones, which they took from the Jordan, Joshua set up in Gilgal.

After the introductory verse the story, as we have seen in other parts of the Elijah cycle, proceeds in three sections or scenes.

The first section (vv. 2–6) is made up entirely of two sets of repetitions as Elijah commands Elisha to stay behind since Yahweh has sent him as far as Bethel, Jericho and then the Jordan. Elisha replies each time with an oath that he will not abandon Elijah. In between this triple repetition comes a double one where the "sons of the prophets" come to Elisha saying: "Do you know that today your master will be taken from your head?" (vv. 3, 5) to which Elisha replies, "I know, be silent!" In Num 11:26f. Joshua also wished for the prophets around Moses to remain silent.

The second section (vv. 7–15) is the main one in the chapter. In these verses, Elisha requests the elder son's portion as his inheritance (see Deut 21:17) and becomes validated as the legitimate successor to Elijah. "This reception of the double share identified Elisha as the first-born among the prophets, that is, as the one entitled to become the new leader of the prophetic guilds in the place of the departed leader" (Carroll: 405). Here, too, Elijah's mantle parts the waters of the Jordan in the same way that Moses used his staff at the Reed Sea in Exod 14:16f. "There is an obvious parallel between the actions of Elisha the successor of Elijah and the actions of Joshua the successor of Moses in the crossing of the Jordan" (Carroll: 411).

The repetition of the crossing of the Jordan brackets this section, along with the 50 men from the "sons of the prophets" who wait for Elisha's return (vv. 7, 16). In the middle of the inclusio Elijah asks a similar question to the one in 1 Kgs 19:20.

2:9	Ask what I may do for you.	šĕ'al māh 'eʿĕśeh lāk
19:20	What have I to do with you?	meh ʿāśîtî lāk

This time, however, the question comes at the end of their relationship, when presumably there is more business between them. In ch. 19, Elisha returned home to slaughter the oxen, feeding the people before returning to minister to Elijah. Now he asks for a double portion of Elijah's "spirit" so that he might continue to minister to the "sons of the prophets" after Elijah is gone. Elijah accedes to the request, if Elisha can pass the tests. It is not enough simply to be Elijah's follower, for Yahweh must listen to the voice of Elisha as he did to Elijah. Elisha is commissioned by receiving the "spirit" of Elijah in the same way as Joshua had the "spirit":

> Yahweh said to Moses, "Take Joshua the son of Nun, a man in whom is the spirit, and lay your hand upon him . . . You shall give to him from your authority, that all the congregation of the people of Israel may obey" (Num 27:18, 20).

> Joshua the son of Nun was full of the spirit of wisdom, for Moses had laid his hands upon him. The people of Israel obeyed him, and did as the Lord had commanded Moses (Deut 34:9).

Elisha's reception of the "spirit" is validated in three places: first, by the test of "seeing" in vv. 10 and 12; second, by Yahweh parting the waters of the Jordan River at Elisha's request in v. 14; and finally, by the affirmation of the community in v. 15.

When he returns across the Jordan, Elisha uses the same techniques as Elijah when he takes Elijah's mantle and strikes the Jordan whose waters roll back so that he can cross over. The main difference in the two crossings is Elisha's call to Yahweh to legitimate the succession of authority. Elisha strikes the water, calls out "Where is Yahweh, the God of Elijah?" and strikes the water again. The waters part and he is able to cross. The waiting community comes to meet and bow down before this "Joshua," affirming him as the inheritor of the spirit of Elijah. These actions confirm the extension of the term "to anoint" in the commission to include Elisha as Elijah's legitimate heir (Carlson 1970: 387–88).

The final section (vv. 16–18) contains a testing of the authority of Elisha's word. The "sons of the prophets" have gathered together 50 strong men (reminiscent of the two groups of 50 prophets Obadiah hid in ch. 18) who wish to look for Elijah. In 1 Kgs 18 Ahab sought "to find" Elijah but could not; Obadiah was afraid the spirit of the Lord might carry Elijah away so that Ahab could not "find" him; and here, Elisha reiterates to these men that it is useless to seek Elijah. Although the community badgers him until he gives in, his word proves reliable as they, too, are not able "to find" Elijah (vv. 17). The test is successful, Elisha's word is reliable, and his inheritance of the "spirit" is confirmed.

2 Kings 1/2 Kgs 8:7–15

> Go, return on your way to the wilderness of Damascus, and
> when you arrive you shall anoint Hazael to be king over Syria.

In this first part of the commission given to Elijah, he is to anoint Hazael as king over Syria. In 2 Kgs 8:7–15, Elisha comes to Damascus and Ben-hadad, who was ill and to whom it had been told that Elisha was a "man of God" (ʾîš hāʾĕlōhîm—used three times), sends Hazael to inquire through him of Yahweh if he will live. This situation can be compared to 2 Kgs 1 in which Ahaziah, king in Samaria, has fallen through the lattice in his upper chamber and sends a messenger to inquire of Baal-zebub, god of Ekron, if he will live. In both places the verb dāraš, "to inquire," is used with the phrase:

1:2 ʾim ʾehyeh mēhŏlî zeh   If I will live from this sickness.
8:8 haʾehyeh mēhŏlî zeh   Will I live from this sickness?

"In this type of divination oracle, the intent was for the prophet (ʾîš haʾĕlōhîm or rōʾeh) to reveal the future or to deliver a decision of the deity in a specified situation" (Long: 490). Long's use of 8:7–15 as the clearest example of the "prophetic inquiry schema" shows that although one oracle was requested (v. 8—will I recover from this sickness?) another oracle was delivered (v. 13—Yahweh has shown me you [as] king over Syria). "The move from an initial narrative tension (Ben Hadad's illness) to its surprising outcome (Ben Hadad's murder) is fully structured by the elements drawn from prophetic divinatory activity" (Long: 494–95).

In the same way Ahaziah sends for an inquiry about his health, which is interrupted by an oracle from Yahweh that he shall die. In 1:3 a messenger (*malʾāk*) of Yahweh sends Elijah (also called a "man of God," also used three times) to challenge Ahaziah's consultation of Baal-zebub with the triple repetition of the question: is it because there is no God in Israel that you have sent to inquire of Baal-zebub, god of Ekron? In 8:10, Elisha reports Yahweh has shown him that Ben-hadad shall die, using the same words as Elijah in 1:4, 6, and 16:

| ch. 1 | for you shall surely die | *kî môt tāmût* |
| ch. 8 | for he shall surely die | *kî môt yāmût* |

And finally, each unit ends with the same words: "and he died, and...became king in his place."

| 1:17 | *wayyāmōt ... wayyimlōk yĕhôrām taḥtāw* |
| 8:15 | *wayyāmōt ... wayyimlōk ḥăzāʾēl taḥtāw* |

Through the parallels between these two narrative units, Elijah and Elisha function in the same role. Just as Elijah had predicted the death of Ahaziah "according to the word of Yahweh" (v. 17), so did Yahweh show Elisha that Ben-hadad would die (v. 10). "Elisha is represented as discerning that the king's malady itself was curable, but that Hazael's personal ambition would result in the murder of the king and the usurpation of the throne" (Unger: 75).

Who was Hazael and why should he be "anointed" as part of the triple commission? The Ben-hadad of this story may be Ben-hadad I who was the son of Tabrimmon, son of Hezion of 1 Kgs 15:16 (Albright: 23–29), or Ben-hadad II who was the Adadidri/Hadadezer of the Assyrian sources (Malamat: 146) of 1 Kings 20/22 who, if these stories are out of place, would have been the son of Hazael (see also 2 Kgs 13:22f.; Miller, 1976: 35) or Benhadad III who was the son of 'Idr and co-regent (Cross, 1972: 42). No matter which Ben-hadad, Hazael "the son of a nobody" (Pritchard: 280) murders him, founds a new dynasty, and proceeds to extend appreciably Aramaean domination over the surrounding territories (Mazar: 144). Joram battles against Hazael in 2 Kgs 8:28–29, receiving the wound which sends him home to Jezreel. "The wounding and withdrawal of Joram and the command of Jehu probably confirmed men in the conviction that the *běrākâ* [blessing] had passed from the king to his commander" (Gray: 544). Thus Hazael's "anointing" affects the balance of power in Israel and sets the stage for Jehu's revolution.

1 Kings 21/2 Kings 9

> Jehu the son of Nimshi you shall anoint to be king over Israel.

The stories about Jehu's anointing and subsequent actions are found in 2 Kgs 9–10, but the sections that tie Elijah and Elisha to the revolution occur in ch. 9. There Elisha initiates the anointing of Jehu, after which Jehu commences the slaughter of the "house of Ahab," killing Joram and Jezebel. There, too, the references to Naboth the Jezreelite provide an obvious link with 1 Kgs 21. The major points of contact between 1 Kgs 21 and 2 Kgs 9 are three. First, Jezreel is the location for both chapters. Second, the property of Naboth the Jezreelite also plays a role in both places. Third, the curses—on the house of Ahab and on Jezebel—are made and fulfilled. The two chapters are different in intended focus, although the dispute over the sale of Naboth's vineyard as it illustrates the divergence between land tenure systems gives strong evidence as to one of the main reasons for the fall of the "house of Ahab" (Miller 1967: 309–10).

Jezreel was an important center, if not the capital, for the Israelite portion of the population in the North. Jezreel may simply have been Ahab's winter capital, but there is evidence in the texts that it was the main residence of Ahab's family (Napier: 377–78). Samaria was crown land, purchased according to non-Israelite legal principles and built to be an independent city-state. Since the land for Samaria was purchased by Omri, and the archaeological evidence shows that the earliest buildings were in the form of a royal quarter, Samaria seems to have been basically an administrative center built in an "enormous divergence from previous traditions" (Kenyon: 82). Samaria was planned with David's Jerusalem model in mind, as an independent city-state having no previous ties to the Israelite governing structures in the North. The traditional tensions between the "Israelite" and "Canaanite" populations there could have been neutralized through a "'personal union,' such as had been practiced in an examplary fashion over a century by the Davidides in Jerusalem and Judah" (Miller 1977: 403). Thus the Omrids chose to go the direction of a radically dualistic solution to the Canaanite problem. With Jezreel functioning as the capital for the Israelite part of the population, Samaria was developed as the next step in a national strategy that provided a consistent duplicate polity—"in Samaria the kings from the house of Omri were kings over the Canaanite portion of the kingdom, and in Jezreel they were kings over Israel" (Miller 1977: 403).

In contrast to the social stratification in Samaria, the ruling class in Jezreel was Israelite in orientation, ruled in the old style through judging by the elders of the community and the traditional land tenure system. The story of Naboth's vineyard (1 Kgs 21) thus becomes paradigmatic for the issues that divided Samaria and Jezreel, king and peasant, "Canaanite" and "Israelite" (M. Cohen: 92). The issue in ch. 21, as in chs. 17–19, is allegiance to Yahweh, focused here over the ownership and control of land. In 21:1–7, there is a word-play centering around *nātan*, whose semantic range covers both giving and selling. Ahab approaches Naboth with a business deal including two options: either a better vineyard or silver for his property. Naboth goes right to the core of the problem as he responds: "Far be it from me, by Yahweh, to sell to you the *inheritance* (*naḥălâ*) of my fathers!" (v. 3). The issue is not over price but over the right of Naboth to continue in the traditional land tenure system. Behaving like a spoiled child who had been denied his way, Ahab reports his conversation to Jezebel saying "but he [Naboth] said, 'I will not sell to you my *vineyard*'" (v. 6). Whereas Naboth and Ahab have understood the grounds for refusal, Ahab misrepresents the issue to Jezebel, who proceeds to act as a queen in a hierarchical social structure. Her response: not to worry, *I* will *give* (*nātan*) to you the vineyard! She understands how to use the power of the throne even if her husband seems reluctant.

21:8–14 contains the account of the trial and killing of Naboth. If Andersen is correct, the strategy that Jezebel used in the trial was a false claim that Naboth had actually promised to sell the vineyard to Ahab and had later reneged. He establishes four advantages for his theory: Jezebel's maneuver was grounded in the known fact that Ahab and Naboth had discussed the deal; it was known that Naboth had invoked the name of Yahweh on that occasion; proof of Naboth's guilt was found in something he is alleged to have said, established by the verbal testimony of two witnesses; and finally, that such an accusation would provide legal grounds for Ahab's seizure of the property (Andersen: 53). Whether or not the Naboth incident actually happened, or that it was the work of a literary artist who wove an exciting story about an event that had taken place long before his time (Miller, 1967: 311), the story revolves around the divergence between two styles of leadership that definitely were at the centerpoint of any discussion about the "house of Ahab."

The continuing aliveness of this issue is indicated by the triple repetition of "Naboth" in the second section of 2 Kgs 9. Verses 1–14a contain the anointing of Jehu—and unlike the previous parts of the commission, this one is a real anointing. After he is anointed by Elisha's emissary and proclaimed king by the people, Jehu is shown in v. 15-28 proceeding to Jezreel to kill Joram. In the same style we have seen before, the triple repetition of *hăšālôm* (Is it peace/well?) provides a dramatic touch to the narrative. When Joram finally comes forth, he and Jehu meet on the property of Naboth the Jezreelite. As this allusion refers to the event portrayed in 1 Kgs 21, the reader/hearer knows that all is not "well," and the stage is set for the final confrontation with the "house of Ahab."

Jehu's answer to Joram's *hăšālôm* is in v. 22b:

> What is the meaning of the question, "Is all well?" so long as
> the harlotries of Jezebel your mother and her sorceries are so
> rife? (Gray: 545).

"Accusations of witchcraft are employed in cases where there are social tensions that cannot be handled by normal rational or legal means" (Wilson: 74). In this case, Jezebel's religious and social power would have continued to be a divisive force in the society even in her position as queen-mother. Because witchcraft accusations result in the fragmentation of a society, they appear when social tensions have reached the point that social fission is inevitable (Wilson: 75). The symbolic meeting of Jehu and Joram on the property of Naboth, and Jehu's accusation of witchcraft against Jezebel give adequate grounds for revolution and the purging of Ahab's family.

The curses which tie together 1 Kgs 21 and 2 Kgs 9 were not part of the pre-Deuteronomistic Elijah cycle but reflect a later attempt to connect Elijah's prophecy against the "house of Ahab" with the actual revolution, showing that "the prophecy which Elijah uttered against the house of Ahab and the fate which Jehu meted out to the remaining members of that dynasty in Jezreel were not entirely unique in the history of the northern kingdom" (Miller, 1967: 319). 21:19–27 contains several curses spoken by Elijah upon Ahab, Jezebel, and the "house of Ahab," two of which are matched in 9:8–10.

21:21	and I will eliminate to Ahab from the males, bond and free in Israel,	9:8	and I will eliminate to Ahab from the males, bond and free in Israel,
21:22	and I will make your house like the house of Jeroboam, son of Nebat, and like the	9:9	and I will make the house of Ahab, like the house of Jeroboam, son of Nebat, and like the

house of Baasha son of Ahijah	house of Baasha son of Ahijah
21:23 and also to Jezebel the Lord spoke saying	9:10 and Jezebel
the dogs shall devour Jezebel	the dogs shall devour
in the property of Jezreel	in the property of Jezreel

The final curse is expanded in 9:36, combining together Yahweh, Elijah, Jezebel, and Jehu: "The word of Yahweh is this which he spoke through the hand of Elijah the Tishbite saying, 'in the property of Jezreel the dogs shall devour the flesh of Jezebel'." Essentially these same prophecies had been uttered against the two preceding royal dynasties, and they had met precisely the same fate (Miller, 1967: 319). Thus even at a later date, the connections between the prophet Elijah, the actions of Elisha, and the revolution against the Omrid dynasty become explicit. Elisha, as a political voice in a time of extreme social crisis, legitimated Jehu's revolution while he himself stood as the authentic successor to Elijah, the prophet who reaffirmed the traditional Mosaic values.

Because prophets speak to specific situations in their society, the prophet, who serves as an intermediary between the human and divine worlds, appears when that society is undergoing stress and rapid social change. In his prophetic role, he articulates the group discontent (Wilson: 28–71). The pre–Deuteronomistic Elijah cycle presents a prophet, Elijah, and his successor, Elisha, combining the religious and social functions of intermediation, reaffirming traditional values while helping to bring about social change. Legends about these two prophets were brought into a written cycle that served to legitimate the prophets' authority and their roles in this revolution against the policies of the Omrid dynasty.

2

The Local Hero in Palestine in Comparative Perspective

SCOTT D. HILL

Introduction

The prophets who appear in the Bible are included there because a tradition has established them as bearers of God's truth. Such claims to truth are not easily made, however, especially when the prophet's message challenges commonly held truths, or regimes in power. Before reaching its final form, truth is negotiated as different groups offer their interpretations of the prophet's "message." A prophet as a canonical figure unifies, balances, and holds in constructive tension various institutions and factions within the tradition. An important part of the biblical account is thus shaped by the prophet's followers and opponents. Knowledge of those followers can help us uncover new facets of biblical texts.

In the case of the Elijah and Elisha accounts, the other essays in this volume establish an origin in "the lives of everyday people" (Rentería), and final incorporation "in a way that gave legitimacy 'without any doubt' to Jehu's reign in Israel" (Todd). This essay seeks to illuminate the social dynamics that shaped that process at many steps in between. It thus shares with those other essays many but not all assumptions about these social settings. In particular, I do not assume uniformity among followers of Elijah and Elisha on any issue or conflict, whether Yahwistic, anti-Omrid, or in favor of any particular class. The unifying factor is essentially Elijah.

The picture we have of any biblical prophet has been shaped from diverse materials on controversial figures by scribes with a definite point of view. Sometimes the scribes succeeded in producing a flat picture consistent with that view. Often they were obliged to leave intriguing loose ends. In any case, politics and issues shaped the message of prophets—during and after their lives—at least as much as the prophets shaped the politics.

The resulting image often portrays a prophet as a lone, God-inspired ascetic. In contrast, I assume that prophets without followings are extremely rare, if indeed any have existed. What are their followings like? What tensions and dynamics shape them? The biblical record offers little help on this question. The biblical redactors usually preferred to depict the truth of the prophets as independent of any social realities, as pure and coming from God alone.

In compiling "scriptures," scribes generally create an ideological arena wherein political, religious, and social institutions coincide with the will of a god. Thus they prefer to omit references to forces that compete with or detract from the centralized authority of the political, religious, and social elite. All biblical prophets are in the canon because they can be seen as, or used in, supporting the Temple or post-Temple cult (a category including Christianity). Some of them might have been incensed at being so used, had they but known. Reconciling this tension generally involves isolating the prophet from all but the broadest social distinctions. Specifically, the prophet must be depicted as favoring the canonizers and opposing their enemies.

Elijah and Elisha are in several ways exceptional. Throughout 1 and 2 Kings, they are tied to the "sons of the prophets" and other groups. Their followers are thus acknowledged to a greater extent than those of most other prophets. In their case, a predecessor of the Deuteronomistic historian is writing to legitimate Jehu's rise. The historian wants to establish a line of authority, a clear path from YHWH to Elijah (via Moses) to Elisha to Jehu. The followers of Elijah and Elisha are depicted as struggling followers of YHWH, dedicated opposition to the dominant Baal worship and the foreign alliances that accompany it. Perhaps this is because the accounts are used to show popular opposition to the Omrids. More likely, they are meant to appeal to certain groups—either social classes or political factions with ties to different classes. The "Deuteronomistic coalition" was probably formed, strengthened, or reflected through the inclusion of these stories and the references to social movements therein.

Yet, even with Elijah and Elisha, the information is neither abundant nor clear. We thus turn to other accounts, outside the Bible. Such accounts of similar "holy figures" often reveal more of the social context than do biblical texts, and careful comparison can suggest new perspectives on biblical prophets.

I set these comparisons in the category of "local hero." The local hero is a man or woman who has been recognized as "holy" in conjunction with shifting balances in social forces. I define holy as having privileged access to power (generally meaning God) beyond the reach of other people. Such "privileged power" often comes in the guise of claims of truth, but it may also be manifested as wonder-working or the ability to overturn a power group. This definition resists the temptation to view holiness, power, and truth as historical or doctrinal facts. That is why the canonical texts are generally not helpful; their job is to establish such facts, not question them. Yet to understand the formation of the texts, we must see that they were in the midst of a struggle of definition. We thus look at holiness, power, and truth as social perceptions. The struggle over control of those perceptions is the appropriate context for viewing the local hero.

Others have taken comparative approaches to "prophetic" literature by studying local heroes from all regions and cultures (Overholt, 1981, 1989). I have restricted my sources for the most part to Palestine and nearby areas. Inhabitants of these areas have long venerated local heroes known by various labels, including saint, *wely*, prophet, and dervish. Throughout history, local shrines to such figures have been important sites for popular worship, practiced either in conjunction with or in tension with the religious system—Jewish, Christian, or Muslim—of the regime controlling the area. For many people, allegiance to monotheistic faith has been less important than their loyalty to the local hero. These heroes range from biblical figures such as Elijah, Elisha, and Moses to more recent saints like Sayyid Ahmad al Badawi, who died in 1276 (Gilsenan, 1973:1) or Sheikh Abu Ghosh from the 18th century C.E. These individuals and their sites of veneration (generally a tomb, but sometimes a birthplace or location of wonder-working) have many similarities to some biblical prophets and holy places. I believe those similarities can lead to productive comparisons regarding the social dynamics of holiness.

Then we can turn to application. In this chapter, I will move from the data on local heroes to suggest some of the social dynamics surrounding Elijah and Elisha and their effect on the accounts in 1 and 2 Kings. At that point, it will be clear that I am not merely taking a hodge-podge of lunatics, saints, and witches and imposing it on Elijah and Elisha, but rather, tentatively suggesting that what institutions and local heroes have been doing for centuries, they also did in the case of these prophets.

Some will be disturbed at the openness and imprecision of this definition of "local hero"—"someone recognized as holy in conjunction with shifting balances in social forces." Yet, its purpose is to provide a broad framework within which all relevant data may be considered. There may be concern that it is impossible to tell from some of my sources whether a figure is really a "local hero." This is precisely the point. Some sources (including the Deuteronomistic History) were written in order to obscure social dynamics and put us at the mercy of their definitions of important figures. I have sought to re-open this data to our use so that we can explore new approaches to biblical prophets. My openness is not indiscriminate; I use this data cautiously.

Yet, where caution is usually used to exclude data, I urge caution against throwing out relevant data because of a particular label, a label that may be used in a polemic (over prophecy and witchcraft, for example) that has been going on for thousands of years. I have consciously resisted creating a new definition with which to filter out data on, say, dervishes and madmen. Instead, I suggest looking at how social movements, factions, and institutions have treated and responded to those who claim holiness. I apply more caution in the analysis than in the definition. Perhaps a rigorous definition is possible or desirable. For the present, I prefer keeping alive important questions about the dynamics behind holiness and authority, including their definition.

Cross-cultural comparisons have their problems (Overholt, 1981). Questions kept alive idly are not the basis for productive investigation. I have taken care not to distort the evidence. Recognizing the potential value of unexamined evidence on local heroes, I have sought to make the evidence available without taking the evidence beyond the limits of its applicability. On the one hand, I have restricted the geographical and cultural bounds for the material (though remaining open to all historical periods), hoping thus to avoid some inappropriate applications. (The reader should decide whether the exceptions, such as material from Morocco, are inappropriate.) On the other hand, I have been quite careful not to assume that characteristics of social institutions carry over from one period, faith, or culture to another. We certainly are cautious in assuming similarities among what the Bible calls "prophets," even those so close in time and source as Elijah and Elisha; the same must hold true for dervishes, *wely*s, Sufis, and saints. We have to look deeper to find meaningful patterns in the social dynamics surrounding holiness, truth, and power.

These similarities can be fruitful so long as we do not try to see them as uniformities. In this way, the broad historical scope of this study is a strength. We can locate common nexuses for the struggle over truth and power that are not bound to specific cases. Their prevalence can suggest a likelihood that their appearance, or sometimes their conspicuous absence, in a biblical text is not coincidental. I do not restrict the picture of the local hero to just those aspects that parallel Elijah and Elisha. This would distort the data. I hope other readers will find connections to explore that I have missed.

The approach I take is somewhat similar to Thomas Overholt's. Both recognize the lack of biblical material on the social context of prophets and compensate for this lack by looking at anthropological data. We both seek to avoid difficulties of such cross-cultural study by focusing on social dynamics. However, what makes these intermediaries comparable for Overholt is that "their chief function is to communicate messages or information from the world of the spirits to the world of humans" (1989: 4). In my study, the common thread is attribution of holiness—also presumably originating with the divine (my examples are exclusively within monotheistic systems) and received in some way by human communities. Rather than a role or function, my focus is on accorded status. I also look less at "prophecy" in words and more at other means of communication and mediation. Furthermore, I devote more attention to the political aspects of prophetic power and to the formation of communities or factions with respect to local heroes. I may thus seem to trust my sources less and to look more at the forces behind and around the text than does Overholt. Thus he passes over issues of tension between the Elijah and Elisha accounts and their redactors that I find important and illuminating (Overholt, 1989: 89, 91).

I proceed to sketch some common features of local hero veneration and how they resemble biblical accounts. I will show what social dynamics they reveal, focusing on four nexuses of authority where power and holiness meet to negotiate truth. Finally, I will see what this study can suggest about Elijah and Elisha. I will conclude by suggesting some metaphors for the local hero's role in social dynamics and areas for further exploration.

The Local Hero

Many writers have noted that modern veneration of holy figures in Palestine resembles biblical descriptions (e.g., Canaan, 1934: 79; Baldensperger, 1913).[1] According to Tewfik Canaan's inventory of "Mohammedan saints and sanctuaries in Palestine," seventy percent of the holy sites were on hilltops (the biblical "high places"), and sixty percent were accompanied by holy trees, much like the descriptions of popular worship found throughout the Bible (e.g., Deut 12:21, 16:21; 1 Kgs 14:23; Jer 3:6–9, 17:2–3; Ezek 20:28).[2] Most of these heroes never become influential beyond their own, or some other, village. The examples we know best are, of course, those with influence on a broader scale (such as Elijah, Elisha, Jesus, Musa as-Sadr of Lebanon, and ʿAbd el-Wahhab, founder of the Islamic Wahhabite movement).

Yet even relatively minor figures are often the most significant religious presence in the lives of villagers and of the peasantry of the surrounding area (Gellner, 1978:308, 318). "There is hardly a village, however small it may be, which does not honor at least one local saint. But generally every settlement boasts of many" (Canaan, 1924:2). His or her significance (it seems most are male) may even outweigh that of God (Canaan, 1934:61), though they are not generally in open competition. The hero may influence the conception, birth, and health of children; the success of crops, business ventures, marriages, and partnerships; safety in travel and work; natural phenomena such as rainfall, plagues, and wild animals. To ensure the hero's favor on their efforts, villagers make sacrifices, pledges, and devotions to their local hero, and burn oil lamps and incense in the hero's shrine.

---

[1] This picture is drawn from Baldensperger (1894), Canaan (1922, 1924, 1925, 1926, 1927, 1934), Conder (1878), Grant (1907), Hanauer (1904), Luke (1927), and Masterman and Macalister (1915, 1916, 1917).

[2] Canaan also notes that 65% of local shrines are located at water sources (1924:42). While he claims that this is consistent with biblical descriptions, his references do not bear this out. In fact, water sources have powerful religious associations throughout the Bible, but biblical sources tend to associate them with Yahweh in opposition to local worship at high places (2 Kgs 23:4,6,12; Jer 3:3 and esp. Jer 2:13 and 17:5–18).

It should be noted that most of the above description applies in the case of heroes living or dead. Whether living or dead, they are similarly venerated, similarly petitioned. They are sought out to adjudicate in similar manners and are believed to wield similar power over human life. After death, heroes may in fact increase in ability to protect people and goods, to kill or injure those who defile their shrine, and to bless their followers. Often living men are viewed as incarnations or representatives of a known local hero.

For a "dead" hero, then, the site of his or her shrine is extremely important as the center from which his power is asserted. The hilltop site and surrounding activities are usually essential to maintaining his role as patron and protector of the village, and perhaps beyond.[3] At the hilltop site there are generally trees, sometimes with fruit free for the picking, provided it is eaten there. The hero protects the site's land and facilities and any goods left there for safe keeping. Some heroes have fierce reputations for punishing pilferers. Once a year, the feast day of the hero comes around—often his birthday (*mawlid*). At that time, the whole village, and sometimes pilgrims from a larger area, come out to feast, celebrate, and make offerings. Feast days are commonly known as occasions for the relaxation of rules, particularly of separation between various segments of society, especially the sexes and classes.

There are many benefits that accrue to those fortunate or wealthy enough to be closely associated with the local hero. Their children, marriages, crops, and business ventures are expected to succeed, and such predictions are often self-fulfilling. The local hero will often act to protect them or their interests.[4] Obviously, they would have opportunities to control access to the holy site. There are other advantages to feeling at home within the tomb or *maqam*. For example, one of the most important means of settling disputes in villages is "swearing," which involves having the accused swear in the sanctuary of a holy figure that she or he had not committed the crime. "Few indeed dare to make a false oath in a

---

[3] According to Canaan, "No place can be considered holy, i.e. inhabited by a holy person, unless two conditions are fulfilled: (1) The performance there of religious acts, such as oaths, vows, lighting lamps, burning incense, etc.; (2) the occurrence there of unnatural phenomena, as, for example, hearing religious music, seeing a light lit by itself, or a severe punishment befalling a trespasser" (1924:46).

[4] The "Laurel Lady" appeared with a sword in the top of a laurel tree in 1917 and repeatedly pushed back English troops trying to take the town (Canaan, 1924:71). Residents of Kiryat Shmona, the Israeli town where Honi the Circle-drawer is believed to be buried, claim that he protected them from rocket fire coming across the Lebanese border during the 1980s (Goldberg, 1988).

shrine, for the vengeance of the saints is most severe" (Canaan, 1926:6). Generally, it is the accuser who is entitled to choose the sanctuary where this will take place, and it is easy to imagine the perceived difference between, for example, swearing in the tomb of a particularly nasty *wely* whose walls had just been repaired by the accuser, or in one dedicated to a good friend of the accused's grandfather. Canaan notes that vows may be made in the name of a living descendant of a *wely* or to servants of a shrine (1926:10). Living or dead, the *wely* or local hero is often at the center of adjudication, of balancing powers. This is possible because his authority derives less from individual acts than from community perceptions. We shall see that activities around a local hero's tomb may be important sources of "otherwise inaccessible power" in villages in Palestine.

Villagers seek any opportunity to please the *wely* or local hero, in order to fulfill their pious duty or to tip the balance in their favor. Among the types of connections which are favored: close neighbors of the *wely* site (Canaan, 1925:180); owners of the property it stands on; relatives of the local hero; anyone decorating the shrine or burning lamps or incense; those who have made particularly large contributions to the site's upkeep; pilgrims visiting the site; the *khaddam*, or servant, of the site, who often lives there; the family of the establisher of the site;[5] and contributors who pay for circumcisions or other ceremonies at the site.[6]

Many heroes do develop a following that goes well beyond the immediate vicinity of their tomb, and doing so means operating at a new level of social organization. To move to status as a hero on a grander scale, the holy figure must serve to balance larger forces than those at the local level. Often this happens as the hero represents the interests of the village against some larger structure or group. The truth that the local hero conveys pertains not only to the cosmic and local, but also to an expanding community, because the message differs either from the *status quo* or from what another group believes. Often the local hero expands her or his following by serving, in effect, as a projection of the identity of some community—whether defined according to geography, economics, religion, ideology, ethnicity, or some combination thereof. Most of the

---

[5] That is, in cases where it is not a traditional burial site—usually a dream or vision inspires the location, as reported by Goldberg (1988) and Canaan (1925).

[6] See Canaan (1926:58), who relates that the event "is thought to be good for both parties. The child is protected by the saint, and the confidence shown in the man of God increases his reputation." No doubt it also ties the benefactor more closely to the *wely*.

time, leaders represent a community in a way consistent with how that community's power has traditionally been viewed, and that figure will remain ordinary and not come to our attention. Beyond the realm defined by "conventional wisdom," however, there always lies an area of unrealized alliances, untapped power, unexpressed yearnings, and untold truth, and it is there that the prophets establish themselves. There are always flaws and oversights in the official explanations of where power and truth lie, and identifying these areas gives local heroes a following that separates them from leaders merely filling an established role. When the local hero finds these "underground" resources, his resulting authority cannot be explained except as divine, or heretical.

It is because the local hero's rise is so much tied to communities that he continues to be powerful after death. This smooth transition suggests that even in life his "success" is less due to his own will than to social forces.

These are the broad outlines of the Palestinian local hero, with the ways his or her holiness is usually manifested. As we move to social dynamics, it is, I hope, already clear from this description how and why local heroes shape, attract, and disrupt groups that may possess political importance. Any such group would desire the favor of "privileged access to power beyond the reach of other people." Alternatively, a group attracted to such a figure (in life or death) would presumably have access to such power and become politically significant, without necessarily any intention to do so. Stuart Schaar has said of the 19th century Muslim world, "Most tribesmen and villagers were ignorant of their potential power through unity.... Except on rare and defined occasions, the ordinary man avoided the perils of proceeding beyond the limits of his local community" (1967:129–30). Somehow, the local hero is or becomes extraordinary and that power is realized.

If we limit ourselves to canonical literature like the Bible, we run the risk of being deceived. Factions and movements have very different criteria for truth and holiness than do scribes, functionaries, and the Deuteronomistic History. Rentería (chapter 3 below) demonstrates that among one audience of the Elijah and Elisha stories, there is a much greater concern for securing bread, oil, and life than for Yahwism. Another group pressed the issue of land rights. It may have been at the final stage that the label "prophet" was securely applied. Prior to that time, their role among competing factions may have quite closely resembled that of people we know only as "false prophets" or "bandits."[7]

The continuity of these social dynamics through time goes beyond specific titles and institutions. The differences and similarities in titles of religious figures can be deceptive. For example, one *wely* may be more like most dervishes than like most *wely*s. Titles depend more on geographical and historical factors than on sociological characteristics, and definition is inevitably a controversial issue. Indeed, definition is itself a part of the history of such figures. A "successful" prophet threatens the existing power relations (mostly by strengthening a group with which he is connected) and thus faces opposition. In response, competing or rival social institutions often give the figure a pejorative label, or define "prophet" or *wely* in a way that depreciates, disparages, and excludes the figure or group in question. In Hosea, "the prophet is a fool" (9:7). Deut 18:9-22 gives a list of forbidden figures, leaving only "a prophet like [Moses]" as legitimate. One person's saint is another's witch or heretic; one's *wely*, another's madman; one's dervish, another's idiot. Ann Wilson Schaef relates similarly that though women today are in relatively little danger of being burned as witches, they have been kept "in their place" by the threat of being labeled "sick, bad, crazy, or stupid" (1981:69). Any title will have its field of meaning shrunk or stretched to benefit one faction or another, and a particular truth-bearer may be described by several different groups in ways that suit each group's interests best, much as Martin Luther King, Jr., was described as a "hero," a "communist," and an "Uncle Tom." To seek merely to "verify" such titles is to overlook an important issue of how groups have granted or opposed his authority.

The question persistently arises: Who is responsible for the continued rise of such figures? Why does their following increase, or fail to increase? Here I mainly pursue the social aspect of this question. The issue of charisma, whether as personality trait or as "true" inspiration, is beyond our reach. We can only judge these figures on the basis of highly interested sources. Yet, the way such sources want us to see a particular hero says as much about the social forces involved as would an "objective" account, and probably more.

---

[7] Conder (1878:227) relates that Sheikh Sibleh and Sheikh Abu Ghosh were 18th and 19th century Palestinian bandits who became *wely*s; Zenner's article on the bandit Aqiili Agha (1972) seems to be describing a process leading in the same direction; Aqiili has acquired certain divine traits.

As mentioned, four factors appear to be particularly crucial, or at least of special interest to sources on local heroes. These factors are their role as building or standing for the identity of a community, their origins (family, village, and region), their use of political and religious structures while standing somewhat apart from them, and their acquisition of divine or semi-divine qualities. Let us observe the role of these factors in the career of one such figure, Lebanon's Musa as-Sadr. "Sayyid Musa" is in many ways representative of the local hero who overturns the established picture of power and establishes himself regionally through being closely identified with a community. This Shiite Muslim *imam* is historically recent, thus in some ways atypical, but he is comparatively well-documented and shows many traits that seem to be common to most local heroes.[8] He came from a powerful Iranian family to an overlooked, downtrodden Lebanese Shiite community that felt little pride in its identity (Ajami, 1986:11). He began by working within the Shiite system, and "during his first decade in the country he worked through establishment politics" (Ibid.: 86). Gradually, by encouraging the identity of a Shiite community whose potential power had gone unrecognized, unrealized, and uncultivated by the political and religious establishment (including other Shiite clerics), Musa as-Sadr set himself apart from those structures. This made him a threat to various interests in Lebanon, and he finally disappeared under suspicious circumstances in Libya in 1978. Since then, many stories have arisen giving Sayyid Musa miraculous powers. While many believe that he was assassinated, many faithful followers have declared Musa the "twelfth *imam*," a legendary immortal figure whose return many Shiites await.

Two brief accounts help explain how Sayyid Musa attracted his following. This first comes from a Shiite lawyer:

> The civil rights of the Shia had been trampled on in Lebanon, he believed. Musa al Sadr's moral authority, the promise of mobilizing apathetic Shia masses that he held out, were the things that swayed this one follower (Ajami, 1986: 105).

The second comes from a Shiite financier:

> It was fear that the financier believed to be the root cause of the Shia dilemma in Lebanon. Sayyid Musa, he said, helped men break with that fear. He credits the cleric with "turning the Shia history in Lebanon upside down." Before Sayyid

---

[8] Much of the perspective on Musa as-Sadr I owe to conversation with Carol and Ben Weir and their impressions of how his authority developed.

Musa, he said, the young Shia were either too frightened to stand up to anyone or were the "tails," the followers, of the leftist parties. The parties led them astray . . . . The parties peddled useless words, he said, words that did not feed or shelter anyone. "We had to get our young people back; no doubt the sayyid did this for us" (Ibid.:109).

Elements of this case that resemble those of other holy figures include Musa as-Sadr's prominent origins, his role as building and in effect standing for the identity of an oppressed minority community, his use of political and religious structures while standing apart from them, and his acquisition of divine or semi-divine qualities.

By serving as a projection of a community's identity, local heroes allow that community to express a power that has lain dormant. In the power structures and common wisdom, the Shiites were an insignificant force in Lebanon. After Musa as-Sadr had empowered them, they had new and surprising power that overturned the reigning conception of Lebanon's power balance. Musa served as the fulcrum that gave the Shiites new leverage, and upon which a new balance might have come to rest. This "power from nowhere" contradicted the previous official version of power distribution; as a result, many considered the power to be divine. (Such shifts in power can just as easily favor a new coalition of the powerful as of the powerless.)

Musa as-Sadr was undoubtedly charismatic and shrewd, and his interactions with many other individuals surely played a role in his popular appeal. In this study, however, I prefer to de-emphasize the individual as a personality with his or her own power, making his or her own decisions. Instead, I prefer to look at the rise of a local hero as a matter of interaction between communities to which they are related. I am less convinced by an approach that suggests it is an individual matter. I prefer to focus more on moves and countermoves by "power structures," finding, as Peter Brown says of late Roman antiquity, that "the historian of the period seldom meets an isolated individual.... For the historian Sozomen, the story of Christianity in Ascalon and Gaza was the story of his own and of a neighboring family" (1981:30). Specifically, as for Sozomen and Musa as-Sadr, community standing is initially and primarily most closely tied to power structures of kinship, and most affected by moves related to those structures.

The local hero often begins to attain stature through family prominence or kinship status. In many eras and cultures, the metaphor of kinship, expressed for instance in such Hebrew and Arabic terms as *mišpāḥâ, hamula, qaraba,* or otherwise, has often been the primary vehicle for, or factor in, political interactions. In fact, it is possible to claim that only the rare individual has had any power outside that of the family. There is, of course, no uniform pattern for how kinship and holy status are related. In some contexts, holy roles are passed on in families, while in others, such dynasties are technically prohibited. The potential disadvantages of coming from a low-status family are obvious, but it has also been fairly common for a powerful family of origin to be something of a hindrance, or at least a complication.

As this effect is both important and somewhat surprising, it is worth illustrating at some length. In fact, the family is only one example of the institutions with which the local hero must be in tension, but a very important one. The first example comes from Abner Cohen's detailed analysis of politics in a Palestinian village (1965). Though it does not involve a local hero, it is still instructive. Cohen tells of the politically decisive friendship between 'Ali Matar, of the Matar *hamula*, and Ibrahim Barham, headman of the Barham *hamula*, the most powerful in the village. Eventually, the Barhams' dominance was overturned by the other *hamulas*. 'Ali Matar, who once gained influence through association with the Barham *hamula*, then gained even more by breaking with it. Ibrahim Barham, meanwhile, found that he had to go down with his *hamula*, for he was a Barham, and could not distance himself as 'Ali could. Despite originally having had much more influence than 'Ali as head of the Barham *hamula*, he lost in the long run since he was unable to adapt to changing political alliances.

This suggests that powerful connections, especially family origins, may be an important factor in determining who can attain local hero status. Even when the hero's origin is a definite advantage, there will often come a point when he or his supporters will want to separate him from it to some extent. In village politics, families often are so embroiled in rivalries and alliances that it is impossible for someone from a powerful family to reach the top. Other families block the rise, to prevent power from being taken from them or otherwise becoming unbalanced.

Evidence of this assertion must of course be indirect. We cannot compile a list of obscure figures who would have become well-known local heroes if not for their powerful families. Cohen's account is suggestive of many others. This is substantiated by looking at long-term patterns in the selection of high religious figures in Egypt (see below). It also helps to explain the tension around issues of family origin evident in accounts of such individuals as Mohammed ibn 'Abd el-Wahhab, Jesus,

Saints Gervasius and Protasius, and local Palestinian heroes. We saw that Musa as-Sadr benefitted from his prominent family at a distance, and this is an even more common pattern, which we will see also in the cases of Shabbetai Zevi and Aqiili Agha. Thus, these and other local heroes are more likely to rise to prominence somewhat outside their village or region of origin. In the instances of dervishes and Moroccan-Israeli Jewish "saints," this dynamic has been institutionalized.

Let us take the example of selection of the rector of Al-Azhar University in Cairo, "the leading religious dignitary in Egypt," as reported by 'Afaf Lutfi al-Sayyid Marsot (1972:150). According to Marsot's list (1972:157), every rector between 1680 and 1838 came from outside Cairo. Despite Cairo's role as the center of power and learning, "the striking fact remains that the leading *ulama* were of *fallah* origin"; indeed, the only family ever to produce three rectors was that of al-Mahdi, not only a *fallah* (peasant) family, but of Coptic descent. Over the long haul as well as the short, those farthest from entrenched power are often more successful in reaching the peak of authority than those who begin closer to it. The rectors in question may or may not be venerated today, but at least for a time they were indeed local heroes. They were attributed holiness, subject to popular confirmation, and often played important roles in balancing powers of institutions and social groups.

Mohammed ibn 'Abd el-Wahhab (born 1703 in el-Uyaynah, now Saudi Arabia) is an example of someone from a powerful family who seems to have skillfully managed the family's good standing to prevent it from becoming a liability (Al-Yassim, 1983). When his religious stands (against veneration of local *welys*, for example) and challenging of local authorities got him into difficulty in his hometown of el-Uyaynah, he was forced to leave (as was his entire family). He studied in Medina and tried to find another town where his family's connections could get him a hearing. Finally, 'Abd el-Wahhab came back to el-Uyaynah, now with standing as a regional religious figure and the support of the town chief. He again reached the limit of respect possible "in his own country," as the local *ulama* claimed he wanted "nothing less than to stir up the common folks to revolt against the authority of the established order" (1983:63). Using his expanding fame, he attempted to build his following from new headquarters in the town of Dar'iyyah in the region of Najd. In this rising military and trade center, the dominant family was receptive to him once he sacrificed one of his principles, namely opposition to taxes. It was to be a good match: Wahhabism became the ideological backing for the expansion of Najdi hegemony and eventually for the unification of what is now Saudi Arabia. (This connection between political centralization and opposition to veneration of local heroes is reminiscent of the Deuteronomists' support of the Josianic reform; see esp. 2 Kgs 23:25.)

'Abd el-Wahhab's disengagements from his family provide an interesting backdrop for the descriptions of Jesus' relations with his family and home. There is much made of his family in the gospels and traditions, and the conflict and tension between accounts indicates the importance with which his family was viewed. There are conflicting genealogies (Matthew 1:1-17; Luke 3:23-38) and birthplaces. Luke makes John and Jesus kin (1:36-42). Luke and Mark depict Jesus distancing himself from his family (Luke 2:48-49; Mark 3:31-35). Similarly, his roots in Nazareth are seen by the author of John (1:46) as hindering him from greater success in a broader context. Yet, family ties also hindered Jesus' success within Galilee:

> Many who heard him were astonished, saying, "Where did this man get all this? What is the wisdom given to him? What mighty works are wrought by his hands! Is this not the carpenter, the son of Mary and brother of James and Joses and Judas and Simon, and are not his sisters here with us?" And they took offense at him. And Jesus said to them, "A prophet is not without honor, except in his own country, and among his own kin, and in his own house" (Mark 6:2–4; see also John 7:5).

Although Jesus is shown trying to distance himself from his family, it is clear that the ties remained strong. His brother James became the leader of the church at his tomb in Jerusalem after Jesus' death.

I would surmise that these irreconcilable accounts show Jesus in the process of walking the same fine line that 'Abd el-Wahhab did. His travels as reported in the gospels could perhaps be seen in a similar light.[9] A degree of fame outside of Galilee may have bolstered Jesus' standing at home. This power in turn could have been turned to his advantage outside the region, but staying too long might have entangled him too deeply in local squabbles, thus producing the mixed evidence we find. This analysis neither accepts nor denies the veracity of attributing these

---

[9] There is not room here to probe in depth the relations of biblical prophets with families, but to show that Jesus' proposed tension stood in a long tradition; see Zech 13:3: "And if anyone again appears as a prophet, his father and mother who bore him will say to him, 'You shall not live, for you speak lies in the name of the Lord'; and his father and mother who bore him shall pierce him through when he prophesies."

words to Jesus. It merely points out a strong concern in the texts and supplies a plausible dynamic behind the portrayals there, with an analogy to another important local hero. There are, of course, other literary and polemical considerations which shape these accounts.

The tension between using an established source of power and breaking with it is repeated constantly in the literature of local heroes. The examples for the family illustrate the broader issue, variously identified as the tension between peripheral and central, prophet and priest, popular and traditional, new and old. Local heroes are involved in change in the sources of truth and power, but always, I believe, with some degree of reliance upon the traditional sources. Any affected groups will be eager to influence the way this tension is resolved into a new balance, and then to keep that balance in place. When a constituency has been identified as a power source, structures develop to manage that source and ensure its stability.

Among the many mechanisms a society develops to hold the new balance in place, the simplest is, again, definition. "Who or what is that woman and why is she talking to all of those people?" The label of saint or witch does wonders to keep things tidy. Whoever has the power to apply such a label and make it stick is able to cue the other players in the social drama to their expected responses: accept, reject, ridicule. This is even easier if tradition designates where holy people are supposed to fit in. Because the "family" is the primary locus of identity and power, the dynasty, with a hereditary holy role, is a common means of regularizing succession and maintaining balance. Because holy dynasties threaten other families, there are alternatives, including orders of monks, dervishes, and Sufis (together not so similar as the heading "order" might suggest), and institutions such as court prophets. These institutions differ from one another, and vary throughout their own lifetime, in terms of where they fit on the spectrum from central to peripheral. Often, the court prophet would be a peripheral element within the center, while a dervish is more likely to be a centralizing aspect of the peripheral.

This is the crucial feature of my understanding of the local hero: that they stand, consciously or unconsciously, at a key point of tension between the center and the periphery of power. This positioning is inseparable from the development of their following. A key point of tension is where the fulcrum must be placed to achieve a new balance. Affected groups in the structures of truth and power will try hard to place them at—or keep them from—such key points.

Points of tension are inevitable whenever someone develops a following. Such a one needs to use the power of institutions; but, as noted, unless leaders set themselves apart from structures to some extent, their role will fit easily within that structure and they will never develop a specific following. Local heroes often unite the community identifying with them largely through opposition to some aspect of the existing, officially "monotheistic" structure. At the least, followers must see their leader as an alternative, or the local hero will not be recognizably distinct from the institutional structures, such as Islam or Christianity.

For simplicity, I will use three rough categories to identify the dynamics surrounding a local hero and the hero's authority: individual moves, institutional moves, and grassroots moves. Any event in which the hero's holiness comes into play or where there is negotiation among groups over the status of the hero will likely involve many levels of strategy, and our materials generally do not spell them out clearly. Often there are several complementary ways of describing an event from the perspective of different elements of society. With these reservations in mind, I hope this division can be a useful organizational principle.

Describing "individual moves" runs the risk of distorting the dynamics because, I believe, most such moves are prompted, invented, or manipulated by groups to whom the local hero represents a threat or, properly used, an asset. We must bear in mind that we know of these figures only through oral and literary traditions with their own axes to grind. Canonical and official literature often begrudgingly accepts that it must acknowledge or even honor a popular local hero who originally challenged institutional authority—or it grasps the opportunity once the hero is safely dead. The resulting record will more often depict a divinely inspired loner than a popular uprising.

Of individual moves, the most dramatic is when a local hero practices or condones behavior that violates religious norms. For example, Jesus, Sayyid al Badawi of Egypt (Baldensperger, 1894:23), Shabbetai Zevi (the 17th century Jewish "pseudo-messiah"), Rashid ed-Din Sinan of the Assassins, and Honi the Circle-drawer were all said to have shown antinomian attitudes. Jesus' conflict with religious law is well known. Shabbatai Zevi "felt it his special vocation to place himself beyond the limits of religious law" (Scholem, 1971:144). "We know that Shabbetai Zevi violated several of the commandments by eating the fat of animals and administering it to others, directing that the paschal sacrifice be performed outside of the Land of Israel and cancelling the fast days" (Ibid.:99). Rashid ed-Din Sinan also attacked the fast, laying out a table for feasting at midday during Ramadan and declaring all present exempt from any religious restriction (Luke, 1927:96). The ancient Honi's transgressions seem to have been more along the lines of neglect or "acting petulantly" toward God (Vermes, 1981:58–82).

Violating the letter of the law is one way for a confident figure to set himself apart from the prevailing religious institution, to put herself right at the key point of tension. If the hero had judged the competing powers correctly (or, as we might especially suspect in Shabbetai Zevi's case, if they had been shrewdly used), he or she would have become the fulcrum for a dramatic new balance. Describing the behavior differently, we might attribute it to the local hero's belief in a higher principle that supersedes the religious code. When that principle is popular, when legalism is generally resented, or when a hated figure can be opposed through the higher principle, then the antinomian act may abruptly increase the hero's following or launch him or her into a broader political or social arena. Of course, the individual circumstances of the time and place will determine whether the prophet's activity merely alienates potential followers or gets him or her executed at any stage of the process.

Thus the institutional and grassroots movers will be quite active using the act to their own advantage. Today we call it "spin control." Institutions may try to provoke the hero into an act they think will be unpopular (for example, the Pharisees in some gospel accounts of Jesus). Grassroots moves would encourage acts they expect to be popular, or perhaps those that would provoke overreaction from authorities. Martyrs are extremely effective saints, and exiles or prisoners have similar appeal.

The key factor in every case, I believe, is whether the hero is at a key point of tension or not. Better yet, one might be at several points of tension. The most important local heroes are those who are put at points of tension that arise after their death because this placement indicates an enduring attribution of authority. Sometimes this happens through application of words or acts attributed to them. Often the figure is said to appear to someone in a later age. In any case, the memory or myth surrounding them has retained (or acquired) potential power to be applied.

Another type of move by the individual is that which seeks to establish his or her neutrality. Neutrality means not only being free from entangling alliances, but also appearing well-suited to an adjudicatory role—playing the neutral judge. As already seen, some heroes establish their neutrality by moving away from their family. By making that move (even though compelled to by social structures), the individual gains more authority as a fair medium for arbitration, one of his prime roles.

Therefore many "holy" figures in Palestine originated outside the region, such as Musa as-Sadr, Shabbetai Zevi, and the bandit Aqiili Agha (Zenner, 1972). For Agha and Musa, the prominence of their families seems to have helped, without compromising their neutrality. For Shabbetai, his family was apparently of no particular aid; most likely he attracted an audience due to the authority of Nathan of Gaza, who proclaimed him the Messiah.[10]

In the case of dervishes, social pressures have ensured that an apparent individual move would be taken to maintain balance and neutrality. The dervish was expected to undertake a period of wandering prior to establishing himself at a shrine (J. P. Brown, 1968:310; Masterman and Macalister, 1916:13–14). It was also expected that a dervish would be descended from the prophet Muhammad.[11] By expecting a dervish to wear the green turban (the symbol of prophetic descent), the community in effect guaranteed the wandering which must have made it possible in the first place, and ensured that any local boy interested in joining the ranks of dervishes would not become a local hero in their village (unless perhaps he was from an already established local hero line). An individual was thus released from the tight controls of the family or kinship structure, and a steady supply of neutral mediators with esteemed lineages was created.

Peter Brown suggests that in claiming neutrality, it is not only family and certain groups that the local hero must hold at arm's length, but even, perhaps, humanity. At least for Syria, "in the late Roman society, the holy man was deliberately not human" (1982:130). The local hero benefits most by functioning essentially as a pawn, merely reflecting a reality of power unexpressed by existing structures. In many ways this is more effective the less human she or he is (and thus the less hampered by family, marriage, wealth, and other human traits that produce

---

[10] It is interesting to note the prophetic pairs that have been linked to one another in Palestine. In addition to Nathan and Shabbetai Zevi, they have included John the Baptizer and Jesus, Elijah and Elisha, Moses and Joshua, the Bab and Baha'ullah. See the discussion below.

[11] John Porter Brown may be contradicting this when he states, "...little was known of his origin and parentage...but these are of little use to a Dervish, who, it is well understood, has no claims to celebrity other than those acquired by his own spiritual powers and personal reputation" (1968:310). Yet, in other places, he reports the status accorded descendants of the prophet.

jealousy and rivalry or that intertwine them in social networks). We shall see that holy institutions are restricted in ways that make them less "human." On the grassroots level, two categories of person are sometimes attributed with holiness because they are well-suited for playing the pawn and already viewed as "non-human": the mad and the dead.

Institutional moves consist mainly of crushing, co-opting, or compromising. Crushing is the most obvious but not necessarily the most effective.[12] If crushing initially fails, an institution must decide whether to apply more force or subtly to co-opt the powerful figure and his or her following. In the ensuing examples where Saints Gervasius and Protasius and Honi the Circle-drawer are co-opted, we see social structures dealing effectively with a perceived threat to their authority.

In *The Cult of the Saints: Its Rise and Function in Latin Christianity* (1981), Peter Brown shows how powerful families and the church hierarchy fought for influence through the medium of saintly remains in the 4th through 6th centuries. The classic example given of the church's adroitness in preventing "the privatization of the holy" by wealthy families involves Ambrose in Milan. The relics of Saints Gervasius and Protasius were discovered there in 385 in a private burial ground, where popular veneration of these two saints was likely to enhance the influence of a powerful family. Ambrose cleverly shifted the relics away from the point of key tension. As Brown explains,

> What was new was the speed and the certainty of touch with which Ambrose appropriated the relics. He moved them after only two days from the shrine of Saints Felix and Nabor, where they had been unearthed, into the new basilica which he had built for himself; and he placed them under the altar, where his own sarcophagus was to have stood. By this move, Gervasius and Protasius were inseparably linked to the communal liturgy, in a church built by the bishop, in which the bishop would frequently preside. In that way, they would be available to the community as a whole (1981:36–37).

In that world, it seems, the saints' cults were a prime locus of power that had to be dealt with, whether as a challenge to the church or one of its pillars. Personal power, especially of Ambrose and the family involved,

---

[12] The lack of data suggests, and it is reasonable to believe, that female holy figures have been the easiest to crush, either as their movement developed or as tradition was transmitted.

was clearly a factor here, but of less interest to us than the impact on institutions. By co-opting the remains, the church directs the saints away from the key point of tension between church and families, advancing the power of both church and saints.

Another example is Honi the Circle-drawer, a charismatic Jewish miracle-worker in 1st century B.C.E. Palestine. He was extremely popular with "the people" but not with the religious authorities; in fact, the leader of the Pharisees reportedly would have excommunicated him if he had dared (Vermes, 1973:81). In following generations, however, it became clear that Honi's fame and popularity were not going away. In fact, his authority as a rainmaker was useful in making the overall picture of rabbis seem more powerful. In response, as William Scott Green has shown (1979), the authorities gradually "rabbinized" Honi, depicting him in ways that fit within the mainstream of Judaism.[13] As with Gervasius and Protasius, the result of avoiding the area of tension is the elevation of the "peripheral" figure in the eyes of the central structure and the elimination of a threat to that central structure's authority. The local hero can then be identified more as an individual example of an institutional role and less as a representative of a threatening power source.

For central structures, co-opting a local hero may be a wiser strategy than being rigidly determined to exclude him. When authorities work too hard to maintain balances, they often suffer in the end. The harder they try to enforce a static balance, the harder it is for forces to shift that balance (for example, the harder it is for Honi to be accepted), but the more disturbing the shift will be when it does come. In contrast, allowing a fluid balance entails less control but leads to many smaller, smoother shifts; the fulcrum can slide slowly rather than jumping abruptly. The fluidity of the power base exhibited in the two examples above prevented too large an opposition force from growing, to be applied when a local hero is well-positioned to act as a fulcrum.

The institutions that work to maintain balance must do so not only by controlling internal movements but also by negotiating a niche in society alongside other institutions. Thus compromise can be an important institutional move. To be granted power in some areas, religious institutions

---

[13] It is interesting to note that Geza Vermes has similarly used a characterization of Honi, along with other figures, such as Hanina ben Dosa, to depict Jesus as falling within the type of charismatic Judaism, or Hasidim (1973:69, 79, 83). In contrast to Green, he argues that this type was "slowly but surely squeezed out beyond the pale of true respectability" (Ibid., 82).

tacitly agree to abstain from seeking power in others. Typically, this has meant that religious figures are expected to practice celibacy, poverty, pacifism, and generosity or hospitality (Kolenkow, 1986; Corrington, 1985; Gellner, 1972:316). Celibacy eliminates the threat of dynasties; more importantly, it prevents local heroes and institutions from building alliances through marriage. Poverty and hospitality restrict those in truth-bearing roles from economic power. Pacifism cuts down one's ability to challenge authority or physically enforce God's will. Consistent with the nature of compromise, we should not take these prohibitions as indicating categorical exclusion from these power sources. What is really meant is that religious forces must work closely with other social structures if they want access to these other forms of power. If they do work with those other structures, the restrictions on them will prove ineffective, as we will see under grassroots moves. The history of the papacy includes many examples of how relative the restrictions on holy power are.

As we turn to grassroots moves, we see that it is not only central structures and powerful families that can manipulate dead heroes to their advantage. Palestinian villagers have sometimes used a mechanism which is strikingly similar to Ambrose's act: keeping the saint's power and reputation for truth from being monopolized by any particular family, especially the hero's own. There are many accounts of bodies of local heroes, while en route to the cemetery, choosing their own burial sites.[14] The pallbearers would somehow be led to a particular site, or the body was described as actually flying to the site it chooses, often a hilltop somewhat removed from habitation (Canaan, 1924:2). In the story of Elijah's ascent, his followers thought "it may be that the Spirit of YHWH has caught him up and cast him upon some mountain or into some valley" (2 Kgs 2:16). The Deuteronomist explains that Moses disappeared without a trace on the other side of the Jordan. These displacements may have separated the hero from his family or other group in order to keep him more neutral. Somehow, as the body was on the way to burial, control over it was wrested from the family and the burial site became situated in a spot where the deceased's following could be greater and where

---

[14] See Canaan (1924:52, 54); Baldensperger's tale of ʿAbd el-Qadr (1894:23); Masterman and Macalister (1916:12); and Conder (1878:228), who also mentions a *wely* whose dog miraculously collects his bones and transports them to a mountaintop—different mechanism, same effect.

more of the village or surrounding region would respect the shrine.[15] The placement of Jesus' tomb in Jerusalem, for example, served to disconnect it from his origins and his followers in Galilee, and possibly expanded the following he attracted.

One case of a displaced corpse offered by Canaan indicates that grassroots and "individual" moves can come to be used as explanations of the same phenomenon. The tomb of esh-Sheikh el–Qatrawani lies on a neutral hilltop outside Qatrah near Gaza. Two stories are told to explain its placement. In one, "he left his village—since he could not fulfill his religious duties there." In the other, the body flew away from the burial procession and landed there (Canaan, 1924:51–52).

As noted under institutional moves, power restrictions on institutions and holy figures (such as celibacy and poverty) are often overlooked. This can also be a grassroots move. Such restrictions cannot simply be dictated; they must be enforced somehow in order to stick, and a local hero with a sufficiently strong movement meets few overt challenges. The grassroots moves behind this and other local hero dynamics are well illustrated by Gellner's description of the *igurramen* or "holy lineages," among the Berbers of the central Atlas Mountains. The saints of these lineages are set apart (in location and function) as mediators and "provide the continuity and the stable framework that the political system of the lay tribes so conspicuously lacks" (1972:315). The selection of individual saints from within these lineages is a model of fluidity used to maintain balance:

> In the local mind...God makes his choice manifest through the possession by the elect of the crucial attributes of pacifism, uncalculating generosity and hospitality, and prosperity. In reality it is, of course, a kind of unconscious choice by the tribesmen which decides the succession. By using this rather than that son, by using this rather than that rival saintly lineage, the tribesmen in effect elect the given son or lineage as the "real" saint (Ibid.:316).

In this fashion, "the people" can determine, even for a religious leader with institutional standing, how large her or his following is, or what degree of holiness they merit. This description of how people may contribute to the authority and truth-bearing of any leader applies to all cultures, but it is rarely so clear and rarely so free to operate as described

---

[15] Both Peter Brown (1981:97) and Gellner (1972:315) refer to shrines set back from towns as good for mediation.

here. This grassroots assertion of support often allows or encourages exceptions to a restriction on the holy role. If the local hero has a sufficiently powerful following, almost any infraction can go unchallenged. Gellner gives an example of how the "obligatorily pacific" *igurramen* carried on bitter rivalries and even seven years of "murderous violence" (Ibid.:322).

The "unconscious choice" (which may in many contexts be at least partly conscious) makes up much of the subtle selection by which grassroots moves use the cult of local heroes. For example, the acceptance of new sites, or the determination of which older sites are kept up and retain their influence, depends on the gradual playing-out of this type of selection. To illustrate, I have selected examples of site change from two contexts.

First, Canaan tells several stories of holy sites that expose some of the factors that go into their selection. "Many places are held sacred only by a few private persons, their renown has not yet spread" (1924:60). Some of these places later grow in standing, while in other cases, their renown never spreads. There are almost no details given that hint at the factors involved, but we can make some guesses. When a poor leprous peasant reported repeated encounters with a *wely* and declared the location a holy site, no one else recognized it (Canaan, 1924:59–60). After the peasant had left the area, the site fell into neglect, and evidently no more was heard from this local hero, perhaps because, as Canaan notes, "he was too poor to offer a light every week, as he should have done according to popular belief." We can reasonably speculate that the visions of wealthier people have been given greater credence.

Sometimes it is easy to see where a scheme may lie behind events that determined the kind of respect accorded a local hero. Some saints have been reported to reject attempts to establish shrines in their name. In the morning, the shrines were repeatedly found torn down and the materials scattered (Canaan, 1924:56), which could easily be interpreted as a message from groups favored by other saints in town. Fearing the assertion of a new source of truth and power, they hoped to intimidate the builders. In one case, the prophet Daniel suddenly changed his mind and asked someone from a nearby village in a dream to build him a shrine (Ibid.:62–63). This is a small-scale example of what I will call resurgence.

A good way for the local hero's reputation to be diminished is if goods entrusted to his or her protection are stolen or damaged by people or animals (Canaan, 1924:36; 1925:173–74)—the schemes of rival families or groups could sometimes lie behind some such pilfering. The hero's power is respected, and his following grows when he demonstrates an ability to punish these infractions. It is easy to imagine that someone with a stake in that reputation could have planted a dead jackal with the tomb's silver lamp in its mouth as evidence of saintly vitality. It is easy to dismiss it as the superstition of the peasantry when human action is labeled divine, but these *wely* battles serve as a device for avoiding overt conflict while working out power struggles.

Second, Goldberg (1988) gives two intriguing cases in which Jewish saints in Morocco changed the geographic area with which they were identified. Some local heroes became "regional heroes"; others were actually transferred to Israel. In the first case, the area revering particular local saints expanded when residents of the surrounding region moved to large urban centers like Fez. One saint became the core around which the city's Jewish community from that region could form, the vehicle by which a larger community could be united. Pilgrimages then began to sites that previously enjoyed only local veneration, and allegiance to other nearby local saints and their sites became subsumed under one, more central figure.

Later, some of these same saints were held to have moved with their followers to Israel, where it seems they have served as symbols for community identity of another sort—the Israeli Moroccan minority. The most prominent examples are from the Avihatsira family of Tefilau. Although North African Jewish tradition opposed such dynasties,[16] the one exception—the family of Avihatsira of Tefilau—produces some of the most widely-respected Moroccan saints. Most notable among them is Rabbi Israel Avihatsira, or "Baba Sali," who moved to Israel before his death and has a widespread following. His living son is a popular religious figure in Israel today, and founded a short-lived Moroccan political party in Israel. It may be that the Avihatsiras had achieved sufficient recognition beyond the Jewish community so that the community could not afford to enforce the prohibition and thereby sacrifice that well-established leadership.

For similar reasons, the leadership of the saints was needed in Israel. Most often, the move was accomplished by the dead saint appearing to someone in a dream and declaring (in Arabic) his intention to move.

---

[16] Goldberg asserts that this Jewish community prohibits succession because their hold on power has traditionally been so weak. I would interpret that to mean that to put such limited power into the hands of one family reduces their flexibility in responding to changing circumstances, which might present opportunities to expand their power, or the need to defend it.

Goldberg relates an incident where a Moroccan immigrant said that Rabbi David Ha-Moshe, entombed in Morocco, had appeared to him and told him that he wished to join his followers in Israel, and henceforth to be venerated at the house of a prominent family in a town outside of Safed. In contrast to Canaan's example of the leper, circumstances, namely one's family's influence, allowed this site to be respected and the move was made, obviously at great advantage to the family and perhaps to the individual (who was not from that family). In fact, the site has become established as one of the stations along the pilgrimage route to the major site of Meron (where 150,000 pilgrims have turned out in recent years).

The Moroccan Jewish saints illustrate the power of local heroes to adapt to circumstances and the changing needs and identity of community. Clearly, the popularity of heroes will wax and wane depending on a variety of factors, but it is generally a primarily grassroots move. I suspect this is especially true of the waxing, or resurgence, of a local hero. By resurgence, I mean a time when the power of the local hero comes back or increases. It may accompany the hero's bodily return. It may come back in a way that eclipses any previous power attributed to the hero. Most often resurgence accompanies a time of community identity crisis (Schaar, 1967:142).

During periods of resurgence, the figure most commonly turned to in Palestine has been the prophet Elijah, a widely venerated hero among Jews, Christians, and Muslims. Believed in all three faiths to have been swept up to heaven in a fiery chariot, and thus to be still alive and capable of returning, his resurgence is best known to Christians in the gospel questions about Jesus' and John's identities (Matt 11:14, 16:14, 17:3–13; Mark 9:11–13; Luke 9:7–8, 19; John 1:21); both Jesus and John the Baptizer were thought by some to have been reincarnations of Elijah. Many Jewish local heroes were linked with Elijah in popular belief, especially Honi (Vermes: 76–77).[17] Jesus was also believed by some to have been John come back to life (Matt 16:14; Luke 9:7, 19). Furthermore, there were the traditions that Jesus himself would return.

Within Islam, especially the Shia branches, there are resurgence traditions about the Mahdi or the "hidden *imam*" who went into hiding and will return to bring justice to the faithful (most believers are "twelvers," who await the coming of the "twelfth" *imam*, who vanished in 880;

---

[17] The Babylonian Talmud claims that Honi returned after 70 years of sleep, but was ignored (Green, 1979:646).

Guillaume, 1954:120). The Mahdist traditions have provided a vehicle for some dramatic examples of resurgence. Many movements have sprung up throughout the Muslim world identifying a local hero as the returning hidden *imam*, most famously Musa as-Sadr and Mohammed Ahmed, the Mahdi who ruled Sudan until his death in 1885.

Cohen gives an example of a political situation that led to resurgence at the end of 1937 when there was a serious armed rebellion in Palestine and the president of the Moslem High Commission was dismissed. He reports that:

> During this period the ritual of the local saints became widespread. Largely under the instructions of Islamic leadership, elaborate ceremonial and ritual activities, on regional and national scales, were instituted. Sanctuaries like those of Nabi Musa, Nabi Rubain, and Nabi Yamin became the centres of pilgrimage for tens of thousands of men, women, and children, from many parts of the country, during special annual seasons which lasted, in some cases, for weeks (1965:13–14).

Although this description is short on details about the forces driving this resurgence, it appears that at least one aspect of it was to assert unified Muslim backing of the Palestinian national movement, and opposition to the British Mandatory government. There are also hints that certain groups gained in prominence within the "Islamic leadership."

Resurgence is in many ways the local hero move par excellence, whether instigated by a central or by a grassroots force. The local hero, being dead, is completely depersonalized, and it is clearly social forces that provide his power; the fulcrum has no mind with which to move itself, but must have been guided by the balancing powers on the seesaw. The ambiguity that always focuses on the hero is here expanded to uncertainty even over whether he is living or dead. In terms of the hero's role as a source or as a conduit of power, we may borrow an analogy from Peter Brown and say that it is unclear whether the hero is "live" or "dead"—the once-dead wire suddenly carries a surprising jolt. Groups or individuals in authority constantly seek, like Ambrose, to "[rewire] an antiquated wiring system: more power could pass through stronger, better insulated wires toward the bishop as leader of the community" (Brown, 1981:37). Although the local hero may appear to be the power source, she or he is more accurately seen as the wire. The *wely* is a versatile vehicle that may be used to complete circuits simple and intricate, sometimes being switched imperceptibly from one source to another.

This may explain why death is no obstacle to their continued functioning; if the wiring is kept in good repair, there will always be sources of truth and power for it to serve.

When we read about local heroes, we should recognize that the phenomenon of resurgence may be troubling to our source, for instance the Bible. If the heroes are "live," the biblical writer must depict them as well-connected to the official power sources. If "dead," they cannot be an important part of those sources. Elijah and Elisha were two such "live wires" that presented problems to biblical writers.

Elijah and Elisha

A discussion of resurgence of local heroes in Palestine focuses inevitably on Elijah and Elisha, particularly the former. Elijah is a powerful religious figure to all three Abrahamic faiths in Palestine, and the hero whose return is most often awaited or reported. He is worshipped at hundreds of shrines throughout the region (in addition to the most famous at Mt. Carmel), often by Jews, Christians, and Muslims together. The power of the legend surrounding him is so strong it has become thoroughly mingled with two other ubiquitous, if less historical figures in Palestinian popular belief—St. George for Christians, and el-Khadr for Muslims.

For Christians and Jews, the resurgence traditions find their basis in (or receive support from) the biblical account of Elijah's bodily ascent in a fiery chariot or whirlwind (2 Kgs 2:11). Having thus escaped death, he has been seen as available for return, even for a kind of reincarnation. Having passed on a "double share of his spirit" to Elisha, he could probably pass some on to figures in later eras, as well. Already within the biblical period, the expectation of his return is recorded in Mal 3:23 (Eng. 4:5). There have been many Jewish traditions and tales about Elijah's return, the most notable that of setting a place for him at every Passover Seder. For Christians, of course, speculation about his return is discussed in gospel questions about Jesus' identity, which also brought in Elisha and John the Baptist in different configurations. For Muslims, the belief is purely popular, as the ascent of Elijah (Elias in Arabic) is not mentioned in the Qurʾan.

Clearly, none of this necessarily applies to the time of Elijah, Elisha, or the Deuteronomistic historian. There is little evidence for these characteristics of Elijah and Elisha prior to the 1st century, so they belong more to the general literature on local heroes and resurgence than to the background on Elijah and Elisha. Yet it is clear evidence of the continuing power of Elijah as a Palestinian local hero. We will never know with much clarity what led to this popularity, but the attempt to investigate it opens up some interesting questions.

If we tried to sketch an outline of Elijah's prophetic "career," it might look like this: he moved, probably in young adulthood, from Gilead to Jezreel. There, as an outsider, he had particular advantages and disadvantages in establishing himself in the community. He made connections there, through his own family or an important family or institution of the area. At the same time, he was able to achieve an arbitrating or mediating role as a neutral outsider. Eventually, his success brought him to a dramatic confrontation on Mount Carmel.

Many alternatives are possible. Elijah may have been a prominent figure in Gilead before coming to Israel. He may have been a leader of a revolt among peasant and "expendable" classes. He may have been a well-known bandit. Finally, he could have been one of the official "priests of the high places" mentioned in 1 Kings. Any of these could lead to a popular following, political leverage, and a role as intermediary. It is unlikely, however, that he was associated purely with the underclasses, because that would have made it relatively easy for him to be crushed in an institutional move early on. His frequent migrations (to Cherith, Zarephath, the wilderness of Damascus) suggest that some group or authority was pursuing him.

Certainly he did not first attain broad notice as depicted in 1 Kings 17. I doubt that a local hero can get very far by announcing a drought and declaring he will not do anything about it for years. The tradents have left much out. It may be that at some point an institutional move was made to discredit him by associating him with the drought. Similarly, we should not assume Elijah won a reputation by being an ardent Yahwist. People were not waiting for "a good Yahwist" to come along and solve their problems—or, if anyone was, they were members of a local elite with an axe to grind.

Elijah's Gileadite origin (assuming this is an authentic detail) most likely helped him to shift some power balances as he developed a reputation. Gilead seems to have been a prosperous area, somewhat on the fringe of Israel, which played a "swing" role in determining who ruled Israel. David, Jehu, and Pekah all prevailed over villainous opponents with Gileadite assistance, although the latter two came after Elijah. Furthermore, during Elijah's time, as the Deuteronomistic historian depicts it, Gilead was a key site of contention among Judah, Israel, and

Syria, and it was in the battle for Gilead that Elijah's rival Ahab was killed. Religiously, the Deuteronomistic historian depicts Gilead as a pocket of Yahwism surrounded by paradigmatic "abominations" (Moabites and Ammonites—see, e.g., 1 Kgs 11:5,7,33). Thus, if he was connected with power in Gilead, Elijah might have been courted for the influence, assistance, or allegiance he could provide from Gileadites.

Why would he have come to Israel? Perhaps he was in exile, having threatened the power structure within Gilead in some way so that he had to flee. Or maybe he was a younger son of an important family who would have had better opportunities in Israel than at home. Yet, most likely is that he (or his family) had fled when Gilead was taken by the Syrians. There may in fact have been a Gilead community in exile.

It is more difficult to sort out the role "Yahwism" played in Elijah's career. It would have depended on the politics of his village or region. If there was an active rivalry between "Yahwism" and "Baalism," he may have had to take sides. It is quite likely, on the other hand, that the village had its own concerns and wanted no part of such disputes. I imagine many peasants and elites saw advantages to them in *nahălâ* (extended household's freehold) and other aspects of traditional Yahwism as described by Todd and Rentería in this volume. Like peasants everywhere, those in Israel were probably leery or resentful of imported customs, but had seen as many abuses in the name of YHWH as any other religious structure. Their primary allegiance was to a local hero (living or dead), especially one who could provide precious water. Much of Elijah's early rise may have been determined by striking the proper balance of local customs, urban Yahwism, and urban Baalism to relate well to various peasant and elite factions. Given that mix, it seems unlikely that he was a straightforward Yahwist for his time. Probably, from his time until the time of Josiah, there was a "wing" of the Yahwists that was more egalitarian and traditionally Yahwist in leaning, and many other Yahwists without any such sympathies. Elijah may have formed an alliance with the former wing, but I believe the biblical account presents an Elijah who has been "Yahwistized," much as Honi was "rabbinized."

The redactors of these texts have also introduced their own attempts to balance religious tensions. For an earlier historian of the house of Jehu, perhaps Elijah's following was too strong to crush, so it was pressed into service to legitimate Jehu. For the Deuteronomistic historian, this meant dealing with the apparent conflict between his attack on all decentralized worship (high places, shrines, and local heroes) and his inclusion of Elijah and Elisha. It must have been a serious dilemma, to which the historian responded by distinguishing them from other local heroes and making them utterly fierce orthodox Yahwists. The conflict on Mt. Carmel is thoroughly anti-Baal, and Elijah is cast clearly in the mold of Moses. Carmel is itself a problem, as it looks suspiciously like the other high places. Finally, there is the issue of control over water sources. As mentioned earlier, Tewfik Canaan and others have demonstrated that water sources are an important part of local hero veneration in Palestine. Yet they are conspicuously absent from biblical passages that talk about hills and stones and trees, implying that biblical writers (and the institutions they represented) kept this important factor exclusively in YHWH's realm. For Elijah and Elisha to show such confident control over rain, dew, and rivers is an exceptional departure. Of course, it is still all shown to spring from YHWH.

On Mt. Carmel, this tension is given fullest expression. Elijah is both at his most powerful and at his most Yahwistic. The episode would seem somewhat authentic; Elijah surely manifested his power against another strong group at Mt. Carmel. The result was decisive for Elijah's career and for the opposition "prophets." Elijah and his forces dealt them a severe blow. Elijah's reputation was firmly established so that the shrine at Mt. Carmel became thoroughly linked to him. It is hard to tell, though, whether the opposition was really "four hundred and fifty prophets of Baal and the four hundred prophets of Asherah, who eat at Jezebel's table" (1 Kgs 18:19). It would have served the Deuteronomistic History's purpose well to depict the battle that way, and much of the tale is clearly pro-Yahwist, anti-Baal, and pro-unity of the twelve tribes.

Mt. Carmel must have already been a significant cultic site at the time of Elijah. If the "high places" proliferated then and thereafter, Carmel could hardly have been overlooked. Probably it was the site of a major hero—the strategic significance and dramatic nature of the location, along a major trade route, would have ensured this. So a battle or confrontation there was a play for the favor of that hero. This could have been initiated by Elijah himself, by a grassroots movement, or institutionally by Elijah's opponents. The sources obviously play down the role of the prior local hero, as well as the supporters ("sons?") who must have helped Elijah kill the "850" prophets (and their followers?).

I feel we must consider the possibility that the living, breathing person Elijah was rendered relatively inactive after the Carmel confrontation, just as his power had reached a peak. He fled and may have been hunted down and killed. This would not necessarily have stopped his following. One miraculous victory against the representatives of a hated dictator, followed by the provision of long-awaited rain, would be enough to provide the biblical material on Elijah. Most of the food-provision stories could have been generated then, or when he was in hiding; or pre-existing stories, including those about other heroes, could have become associated with Elijah. The only accounts that follow Carmel in 1 and 2 Kings are those dealing with Naboth and Elisha. Todd and others have shown that the Jehuid historian had adequate motivation to fabricate most of this material, with clear reference to Moses, in order to establish the flow of authority: YHWH to Moses to Elijah to Elisha to Jehu. This leaves only the denunciation of Ahab over Naboth's vineyard, which could easily have predated Carmel.

Our interpretation of the Ramoth-Gilead battle account may determine our opinion of the timing of Elijah's death. First, in the long debate over whether to attack or not, why is Elijah never mentioned? He would have been a prominent prophet, and one with a definite interest in the fate of his homeland, yet he evidently said nothing. It could be that he was not consulted because, as a Gileadite, he was considered biased. He may have supported the decision to attack, and the redactors chose to leave out this embarrassing detail. Or he may have been dead. In any case, the death of Ahab at Ramoth-Gilead would have done much to boost the legend of Elijah, and his continuing power.

Why would not the death of Elijah have been acknowledged? This can be analyzed in terms of institutional and grassroots moves. The institutions opposed to Elijah may have been happy to announce his death, but reluctant to turn over the body to prevent the martyr and his shrine from attracting more support. The opposition may have been divided, some wanting to insist he still lived, others hoping to use his death as a rallying point. Even if the body was available to them, grassroots efforts may have been in dispute or confused over where he should be buried, where it was shrewdest or most appropriate to establish his tomb. There may have been some unsuccessful attempt to move his body in a "flying corpse" fashion, to a prominent or strategic location. The body of a Sufi master (Muhammad al-Jazuli in the 15th century) was once carried between guerilla bases in Morocco for 20 years before being buried in Haha and uniting the tribes behind his cause. The situation in 2 Kgs 2:16–18 could be read back into this time. Perhaps the issue was never settled, or it was agreed that his body had been swept into heaven by a whirlwind without him dying. Thus, death may have made Elijah a better leader and unifying force, as his legend could become more polyvalent, seeming to stand for different things to different groups at the same time.

As stated earlier, a movement or coalition can often use a martyr or an exile more effectively than a living hero. Ahab cut the conduit of power, only to find that he freed it to hook up to a higher voltage.

The Jehuid historian's goals were clear, as laid out by Todd: to use Elijah to legitimate Jehu. The Deuteronomistic Historian was making an exception for Elijah in lifting up that local hero. On the one hand, it was to legitimate Jehu. On the other, Elijah's popularity may have been such that it was easier to co-opt than to crush. Or, Elijah may really have been such a clear example of a pro-Yahwist leader that he was an appropriate model. In any case, it was best to portray his passing on power to Elisha through showing a revelation (at Horeb, a good Yahwistic site) and a long period of overlap between them. Finally, Elisha's witnessing his spectacular ascent laid to rest any speculation about Elijah's corpse. Again, this was an act of YHWH—well over the head of any grassroots movement or institution's ability to use him. It took the issue out of the realm of other local heroes, just like distinguishing "a prophet like Moses" from other prophets.

Thus, I find it likely that Elijah and Elisha never met. If Elijah had lived to see Ahab's death at Ramoth-Gilead, would this not have been noted somehow in the text? Elisha was a player in regional politics who somehow became connected with the cult of Elijah—by an individual, grassroots, or institutional move. The connection could have originated with the Deuteronomistic historian, but I doubt it; it goes back at least to the Jehuid historian.

Their relationship may be part of another interesting pattern: prophetic pairs in Palestine. The evidence is intriguing, but not very conclusive. Among well-known figures, we can identify the following pairs: Moses and Joshua, Elijah and Elisha, Jesus and John, the Bab and Baha'ullah (leaders of the Baha'i faith), and Nathan of Gaza and Shabbetai Zevi. The danger in accepting this data is clear: Elijah and Elisha are more or less the key to the set. They are in many important ways patterned on Moses and Joshua. By creating this connection, the Deuteronomistic historian probably paved the way for the analogy with John and Jesus. This leaves us with only the Bab and Bah'ullah, plus the much less convincing case of Nathan and Shabbetai Zevi. I could find no clear example of this phenomenon among the lesser-known local heroes. Finally, the corollary evidence is mostly negative—tombs and shrines of these pairs are not linked, and the Qur'an makes no connection between Moses and Joshua (the latter not being mentioned), nor between Elijah and Elisha. The evidence for a pattern of prophetic pairs is thus intriguing but, on the whole, uncertain. The related cases cast no light on Elijah and Elisha's relationship. We will return to this question after a brief look at Elisha's career.

It seems well-accepted that Elisha carried even more weight in official circles than Elijah had. He actually anoints the kings; he also provides water to armies, heals Naaman, commander of the Syrian army, and spies on Syrian troops for the king of Israel. His popularity among other groups is less certain. The biblical accounts seem to put him in closer contact with the "sons of the prophets," and there is no reason to doubt this. Even more than with Elijah, it is easier to imagine Elisha's "peasant origins" to be literary fiction than literal truth. The account in 1 Kings 19 is sketchy, very briefly mentioning "ploughing," and the scene seems to have been created to link Elijah and Elisha; there is no serious attempt to depict Elisha as a peasant, and the circles he moved in suggest he was born to influence.

The connection to Elijah probably developed later. Somehow, he was evidently in a position of intermediating between factions in a time of shifting power. In that capacity, he was sure to have contact with "sons of prophets." We cannot say whether this group was (or these groups were) more of an institution or a grassroots coalition, nor can we claim with any certainty whether Elisha rose through their ranks, fought for their cause, or merely worked with them as a power broker. Quite possibly, he was somehow in a position whereby he cut a deal between a regime in growing need of broader support and a movement of increasing influence. In the process, he gained the respect and/or appreciation of both sides. He opened up possibilities for hope among the sons of the prophets and their constituency, and probably found ways to provide food for them as well. It is highly likely that Gilead was also a factor in his intermediation.

It is possible, then, that Elisha (in an "individual move") declared his intention to work against Joram by "taking up the mantle of Elijah," perhaps in an appearance on Mount Carmel (though the appearances of Elisha at Carmel may have been invented by the Jehuid historian or an earlier source). It is even conceivable that he emerged from activity in Gilead, crossed the Jordan, and rallied support in a march to Carmel; or that the sons of the prophets or other Elijah followers encouraged a symbolic movement to capitalize on Elijah's solid authority.

Was Elijah's authority that solid? As I have outlined his career here, the figure of Elijah almost seems to shrink before our eyes. His life as a prophet has been nearly reduced to meddling in regional politics, one impressive battle with ensuing rain, and an early death. Can this explain the biblical record and the enduring significance of Elijah the prophet?

I feel it can, if we are willing to grant the authority of Elijah the prophet some freedom from the life and death of Elijah the man. His authority in his time owed much to individual moves well measured against institutional and grassroots moves around him. His long-term importance may have much less to do with how he lived than where and when. In fact, the confrontation on Mount Carmel may have sealed the fate of Elijah the man while ensuring the vitality of Elijah the local hero and his cult.

Mount Carmel may really have been the first step for Elijah the "global hero." Tied now to a powerful cult, known for a successful act of defiance, and, most importantly, given responsibility for ending an awful drought, Elijah has given the people of Israel something to run with. His ensuing "disappearance" would have both spurred the rumors and left his reputation more free-floating. This period may be the most likely time for the origin of the "provision" stories. Elijah could appear anywhere now. Rentería (Chapter 3 below) points out the "empowering" nature of these stories; that fits well with a powerful prophet whose movements and acts have become subject to the will of the people (although the literature I have cited does not include acts of power of quite this nature—they are more of protection than provision). In fact, the nebulous origins and unpredictable whereabouts of the biblical Elijah are reminiscent of many other local heroes, including some who appear in tales of heroes born centuries later. It tempts me to wonder whether he was indeed "alive" even in the time of Ahab, or whether it was his presence that was given credit for miraculous events in those days.

Thus Elijah was available as a power source in the time of Elisha and Jehu. After Elijah figuratively "anointed" Jehu, was he called on to legitimate the regime in other ways? Was Jehu actually fervently anti-Baal, and did he carry out his massacres in the name of Elijah? Did Elijah become an "official" hero years later under Hezekiah and Josiah, a controlled outlet for practices they crushed at unauthorized high places? There must have been official expression of Elijah's "preferred" status beyond just scripturally co-opting him. We may never know when the "Yahwization" of Elijah began, but it is clear that his appeal and usefulness did not end with his death. Yet, as he helped Elisha and Jehu, it may be that they actually made him a "global hero."

Conclusion

To understand the local heroes we must focus on their ability, not to generate power, but to carry it. Elijah was a wire. He illustrates that a local hero is powered by "voltage"—also known electrically as "potential difference"—a measure of force needed to carry current against resistance. In electricity, if the voltage is high enough and no wire is provided, the current will find a path, discharging sparks to equalize the imbalance. In Palestinian history, the gap has been bridged with heroes like Elijah.[18]

The outline here of that process is somewhat sketchy and speculative, but it illustrates the potential for applying the knowledge and perspective gained by studying local heroes. The prophet carries power, and if we look carefully, we can see the hands trying to connect them and direct the flow.

A local hero is also a wild card. In the community's battles over truth and power, the hero, especially the dead *wely* or saint, is available unexpectedly to shift the balance—not by creating a new hand from thin air, but by allowing a fairly good hand to become better by extending a straight or flush. Over the long term, it may be that the local hero plays a variety of roles in a variety of hands without seeming to favor any particular institution or faction. However, wild cards are likely to help out most often those players holding the "aces" of truth—the central religious and political authorities—but to be most dramatic when miraculously transforming a seemingly weak hand. Though the deck is normally stacked in favor of those central powers, the local hero calls their bluff and lets each community's hand, or power, be evaluated in a new way. The figures profiled in this essay are those sometimes used as alternatives to officially decreed truth. A shrine may go through periods when it does not function as a significant "religious figure" or local hero, only acquiring a dedicated following when needed—when someone has challenged the conventional wisdom on how things have to be. Those challenges to the conventional wisdom and the communities that respond to them take highly diverse forms.

Often, it is not the hero/wild card that makes the hand, but the hand (circumstances and coalitions) that makes the hero. Elijah's power and authority were based in groups desperately threatened by drought and

---

[18] A thorough study of devotion to Elijah in Palestine has been done by Augustinovic. He reports that some Palestinians even merge the names of Elijah (Elias) and el-Khadr ("the green one") and refer to "Khidrlas."

by the Omrids. Within the growing anti-Omrid base there were significant groups of Yahwists, and those who favored traditional local systems of land tenure, agriculture, governance, and cult. There were others who felt that any change would present an opportunity for personal gain. In addition, there were Gileadites and particular factions of Gileadites. Each group was sure that Elijah was just the card they needed to complete their hand. Yet, some agent served to keep his power and his legend from remaining the property of any one group. Such an agent may not have been apparent during the life of Elijah himself. I suspect this role for Elijah became clearer during the time of Elisha, especially after the rise of Jehu. It would have continued to take on new dimensions during and after its shaping by the Jehuid historian and his successors. Who was the most important agent in Elijah's career: Elijah himself, a power broker of his day; Yahwistic values; empowered peasants; local elites; economic forces; Elisha; Jehu; Ahab's and Jezebel's miscalculations; Gileadites; the Deuteronomistic historians and their coalition; or the divine will? Whatever the interpretive bent of the reader, I believe the questions raised and the models put forward here contribute to a deeper and more comprehensive understanding of how it came about.

Some readers will have reached this point still waiting to be presented with a clear pattern of how holy status is attained, or a detailed analysis of the factors favoring and hindering the rise of particular prophets like Elijah and Elisha. They may be disappointed, for the possible routes to authority are varied, and the details of each case vary as well. The nature of power and holiness do not allow such a reductionist model. Nor, if we had it, would it be easy to apply, thanks to our sources. What we do have is a better understanding of the social dynamics of local heroes, laid out in a rough profile, a model of a floating fulcrum, and the metaphors of wiring and the wild card. These allow us to focus on productive areas of inquiry, suggesting new meaning to what is written and helpful clues as to what may have been left out—the latter an essential consideration. Our exploration of Elijah and Elisha illustrates clearly that the perspective we gain from disciplined comparison with related figures can have an important effect on the way we look at prophets and the biblical accounts concerning them.

3

The Elijah/Elijah Stories: A Socio-cultural Analysis of Prophets and People in Ninth-Century B.C.E. Israel

TAMIS HOOVER RENTERÍA

Introduction

The Elijah/Elisha miracle stories, when placed in socio-cultural and historical context, enable the modern reader to cut back through time and text to a layer of cultural experience not easily glimpsed through the various editions making up the biblical text—to an anti-monarchic tradition. The stories reveal their resistance to monarchy at several different levels. First, they reflect the experiences of women and peasants in 9th century Israel, two groups that suffered most under the Omrid dynasty. Second, the stories depict these people empowering themselves through transactions with prophets, a type of interaction that intrinsically challenged state power. Third, the stories demonstrate how prophets like Elijah and Elisha, heroes of the hillcountry, may have gained popularity as alternative power sources to the monarchy. And finally, their narrative form indicates that these stories may exemplify a genre wielded in interclan political struggles that threatened monarchic stability (see Hill, Chapter 2 above).

These anti-monarchic tales told about Elisha and Elijah are of two types. The first type suggests by its complex form and sophisticated political content a use and origin as political propaganda in written form. The second type, with which this analysis is concerned, features a form and content suggesting an origin in oral story-telling.[1] These latter stories, with their simple narratives depicting the prophet interacting with a single group or individual, intimate a social world outside the monarchic circle and in fundamental conflict with it.

Why such hill-country oral traditions depicting the lives and realities of village people and their local heroes were incorporated into state legitimation narratives about central kings and elites is an intriguing question. The answer requires an understanding of the strategic dynamics of monarchic power in ancient Israel. First, it is clear from the biblical record that a king or aspiring monarch in Israel had to shape his politics within the constraints of both the encompassing Near Eastern arena and the local Israelite scene. On the interstate front, he jockeyed with other kings and states over trade routes and cities. On the intrastate lines he wrestled with fellow elites and clans over land and political supremacy.

What is not obvious is the details of how a man gained power for himself and his clan. Biblical texts indicate that men became kings in Israel when they managed to link themselves with a powerful Yahwistic prophet. This essay builds on that idea by suggesting that miracle stories about prophets played an integral part in interclan struggles for power. Sparring factions brandished these stories like weapons, making political claims on each other through the language of Yahwism. Each group promoted its own prophet as the true representative of Yahweh, and thus advanced their own clan or faction as the one legitimized to monopolize power.

In his bid for monarchic power, Omri chose to reach outside of this context of interclan bickering by forming political and economic ties with non-Israelite groups. Instead of playing by Israelite rules and using the language and cultural forms of Yahwism to legitimate his dynasty, he and his heirs suppressed this traditional form of political/religious struggle by making international alliances and importing foreign cultural forms like Baalism. Using this strategy against their elite rivals, they maintained power for several generations.

---

[1] Both the origial idea for analyzing these stories as oral tales and the general understanding of Israelite social dynamics owe a great deal to Marvin L. Chaney's unpublished lectures at San Francisco Theological Seminary and Graduate Theological Union.

However, Yahwistic practices simmered in Israel's hillcountry, bubbling with stories of prophets like Elijah who fed the hungry, empowered the poor, and challenged kings with their Yahweh-derived authority. Eventually, the clans and factions behind Jehu, a captain in the Omrid army, harnessed these stories to legitimize their rival claim to the monarchy. Unlike the Omrids, the Jehu party worked within Yahwistic cultural forms. They courted their rivals with stories about the power and authority of their patron prophets, Elijah and Elisha.

Whether or not the actual historical figures of Elijah or Elisha were involved in any anti-Omrid movement is difficult to ascertain. However, as Todd argues (Chapter 1 above), the stories about these prophets were incorporated into a cycle of written tales supporting Jehu's coup d'état. The probability that they were selected for such a legitimation document suggests that they were politically-charged narratives bolstering Jehu's claim to the Israelite kingship. Their inclusion indicates that Jehu's revolt depended on a broad base of support since these stories reflect not only the concerns and experiences of Jehu's elite rivals and allies, but also those of some of the least powerful people within the kingdom.

It seems clear why the longer stories, depicting Elijah and Elisha with kings, armies, priests and other elites, were included in Jehu's narratives. By thus reorganizing and coopting these tales, Jehu staked out his Yahwistic authority over the other clans. However, why the shorter stories showing the prophets with common women and peasants were included is more difficult to explain. First, they illustrate some of the distressful conditions suffered by the powerless under the Omrids, and probably throughout the monarchy, even under Jehu. Second, they depict the difficulties of women's lives under two kinds of patriarchy, the monarchy and the village clan, neither of which was likely to have changed with the shift of regime to Jehu.

In order to discover why Jehu included such stories in his legitimation documents, it is necessary to understand the social dynamics surrounding their generation and reproduction. This task requires a broad historical view that employs the insights of both social and cultural anthropology to outline the probable social dimensions of 9th-century northern Israelite life. Accordingly, this essay begins with a brief description of its theoretical framework, followed by a discussion of the historical context of the stories. This historical section is divided into two parts. The first describes the relationship of northern Israel to the wider Near East during the 9th century. The second describes the internal dynamics and problems of the kingdom of Israel during the same period (following

Bright, 1981). The discussion then moves to the stories themselves, demonstrating how they evidence everyday life in Israel under the historical constraints described in the first two sections. These stories reflect the experiences of people looking for alternative power sources from those offered by the Omrid state, and give a glimpse of how and perhaps why oral sources of prophet-centered Yahwistic resistance were incorporated into the monarchic literature of the state.

The last section pulls together the threads of the entire analysis by discussing power dynamics involved in the production and reproduction of these stories in 9th-century Israel. This includes an analysis of how these stories, both as representatives of a genre and as historically specific tales, can be considered a literature of monarchic resistance.

Theoretical Framework

This analysis assumes that biblical texts are the products of particular social contexts, the expressions of people's experiences under specific socio-historical conditions. It is informed by such works as Chaney (1982, 1983), Frick, Gottwald (1979), and, concerning the broader context of these prophetic stories in the Bible's traditional history, Coote and Coote. Their interest in social context and power, like mine, is grounded in a shifting Christian theological hermeneutic, influenced by post-'60s changes in middle-class mainstream churches that include a burgeoning awareness of social inequality and Third World issues.

Recent directions in cultural anthropology can yield further insight into the social contexts of biblical texts by combining interpretive approaches to culture with analyses of power. My own approach combines biblical studies, social anthropology, and current post-structuralist trends in interpretive historical-material anthropology.

The social anthropology I employ in this paper includes state formation theory, peasant studies, comparative analyses of agrarian societies, and transactional political anthropology. I use these primarily to reconstruct the Israelite social structure in the 9th century B.C.E., as well as to understand the larger Near Eastern system that encompassed Israel. In addition, I use comparative work on transactional power relationships for analyzing the stories, as well as their possible use in clan political struggles (cf. F.G. Bailey; Comaroff, 1978; Kapferer).

However necessary such structural analysis is, it is difficult to capture the life and spirit of a people using materialist, structural-functional, and comparative analyses. States may evolve similarly, peasants may react to certain conditions in somewhat predictable ways, and agrarian societies may be structured according to certain patterns, but each people has its own way of responding to these structural limitations and pressures, and its own way of expressing how it feels to live under these conditions within particular historical circumstances. Similarly, transactional group relationships may appear comparable across cultures, but the meanings attached to them may be dissimilar. Structure cannot explain everything about content, nor the detailed particularities of the meanings that people attach to what may be similar structural relationships (cf. esp. C. Geertz).[2]

Recent trends among cultural anthropologists concerned with the relationship of meaning to structures of power have sought to synthesize cultural analysis with social, political, and economic anthropology, creating new forms of "culture and power" interpretive analysis. This movement also embraces an increased interest in textual criticism, history, and gender studies (see M. Z. Rosaldo, R. Rosaldo, Ortner, Ortner and Whitehead). In keeping with these directions, anthropologists like myself, who are steeped in historical-material discourse, have gravitated toward cultural theorists like literary critic Raymond Williams and historian E. P. Thompson (1963, 1978).

William's concept of "hegemony" as a way of thinking and feeling that saturates the everyday lives of particular peoples and that is shaped by a specific experience of power provides a way to avoid both undue structural–functional reductiveness and the rigid models employed by much social analysis, while still interpreting the experiences of people in terms of the power relationships that constrain their lives.[3]

> It is a whole body of practices and expectations, over the whole of living: our senses and assignments of energy, our shaping perceptions of ourselves and our world. It is a lived system of meanings and values... It thus constitutes a sense of reality for most people in a society, a sense of absolute because

---

[2] Geertz's interpretive method, "thick description," however, lacks a method for understanding the way relationships of power affect culture, and furthermore, has limited usefulness for the study of "dead" cultures like those reflected in the biblical texts, which cannot be observed in action.

[3] Williams and Thompson, like many contemporary anthropologists, oppose the rigid simplicity of theories that attempt to explain all human behavior and expression according to predictive, structural-functional models that leave no place for human agency or subjectivity. Thompson (1978) critiques structural Marxism of the Althusserian variety, for which see Althusser, and G. A. Cohen. A current approach to the problem of agency is proposed by Bourdieu; and cf. Willis.

> experienced reality. . . . It is. . . in this sense a "culture," but a culture which has also to be seen as the lived dominance and subordination of particular classes (Williams: 10).

Both Williams and Thompson argue that history is a *lived social process* in which the way a human being makes a living cannot be separated from the way he or she thinks about life. People make choices about the way they live within the constraints of involuntary changes in the mode of production and societal responses to such changes (Thompson, 1978: 266). These constraints shape the particular hegemony of their lives.

The Elisha and Elijah miracle texts lend themselves well to an analysis of such hegemonic dynamics in Omrid Israel particularly in three areas of current concern in cultural anthropology. The first is the study of the struggle between dominant hegemonies and resistance to those hegemonies, what Williams calls "counter-hegemonies" (Williams: 110–14). In Israel, the conflict festered between a centralizing monarchic hegemony and a regional village counter-hegemony. It began in united Israel with the first king, and continued in northern Israel, erupting at intervals, until the Assyrians destroyed the monarchy in the 8th century. In the 9th century, the period that concerns this analysis, the Omrid kings maintained policies which strengthened the dominant monarchic hegemony, and, in response, the regional village counter-hegemony waxed increasingly resistant until the Jehu revolution overthrew the Omrids.

Both the dominant hegemony and the counter-hegemony in Israel were ways of life that made intimate, practical sense to those participating in them. However, the monarchic hegemony, based on an agrarian state political economy and dabbling in cosmopolitan values, threatened to absorb and completely subordinate the hill-country life of Israelite villagers, who shared political-economic practices and a tradition of Yahwistic history. This increasing power of the state to encroach on village life in the 9th century was rooted in wider changes in the political economy of the Near East. Some of the effects of this changing mode of production on the villagers and common people of Israel can be glimpsed through the Elijah-Elisha miracle stories, providing evidence of resistance to the state hegemony. Furthermore, such resistance indicates what the dominant hegemony of a centralizing Israelite monarchy had to contend with in its struggles to absorb and assimilate rural regionalist Yahwism.

This is an example of what Williams means when he suggests that dominant hegemonies must "continuously be renewed, recreated, defended and modified" (Williams: 112–15). Those who benefit from hegemonies constantly jockey their positions to incorporate and absorb cultural elements which challenge their dominance.

Israelite resistance embraced not only political movements like that leading to Jehu's revolt, but also less obviously defiant cultural practices, rooted in the daily lives of hill-country villagers. The analysis of such everyday practices of resistance is another area of current concern in cultural anthropology (e.g., Comaroff, 1985; Price; Scott; Taussig). In the case of village Israel, this included the practice of relying on local Yahwistic prophets, or, as Hill calls them, "heroes" (Chapter 2 above), to link people with supernatural powers, rather than trusting a monarchy that claimed to control the rain and supply subsistence, and yet failed to do so. Whether or not these practices were explicitly anti-monarchic or anti-Omrid—that is, understood by the social actors themselves as resistant—is impossible to know. However, the fact that the relationships as documented in the stories reflect a non-monarchic culture, particularly since they were preserved within a monarchic literature, makes them "counter-hegemonic."

Furthermore, the probable use of the prophetic genre in living oral warfare between clans, was itself a practice resistant to monarchic attempts at monopolizing power in two different senses. First, the practice was tribal and regional, threatening the creation and maintenance of a monarchic state by leaving power up for grabs in struggles between clans. Omri tried to circumvent this by putting himself out of the clan arena through foreign alliances.

Second, the practice as it continued even after Jehu's coup threatened all monarchic claims to power because it left open the question of who the most Yahwistically legitimate family to rule was. Jehu attempted to consolidate his authority by commissioning a public narrative that authorized him as a king anointed by the most authentic spokesperson of Yahweh, Elisha, successor to Elijah. In this way he attempted to legitimize himself within hill-country traditions. However, he was unable to suppress completely the Yahwistic practices of his subjects, whether elites or peasants, and prophetic stories continued to circulate as a genre of monarchic resistance.

In another vein, the stories demonstrate resistance through the presence of women characters who feed and shelter prophets while negotiating with them to provide things the women desperately need. At one level, the women depicted demonstrate resistance simply in their support of Yahwistic prophets, just like the men in the stories. But a closer look at the stories in terms of gender dynamics suggests that women may have been reaching out to prophets out of their sense of subordination as women. They were vulnerable not only within the monarchic system, but also within the traditional Yahwistic village system, since both were patriarchal.

The question of Israelite gender dynamics belongs to another arena of current anthropological interest, the relationship between gender, culture, and power. Many recent approaches suggest that the dynamics between different hegemonies, as well as between dominant hegemonies and counter-hegemonies, cannot be fully understood without examining the cultural construction of gender embedded within them. In other words, power inequalities structured by unequal access to the means of production cannot be understood apart from the dynamics of gender (cf. C.W. Bailey; Collier and Rosaldo).

Thus, in terms of theoretical issues, from the perspective of critical cultural anthropological analysis, the Elijah-Elisha literature as excavated through form-critical analysis provides a case study for the analysis of the dynamics between a particular *dominant hegemony*—the Omrid, agrarian, internationally oriented urban state and the literature they produced to legitimize themselves—versus a particular *counter-hegemony*—Elijah/Elishian prophetic, Yahwistic, regional, rural, traditional relationships and the stories they produced. It also furnishes a glimpse into the nature of gender dynamics in ancient Israel, a hegemonic tension that cut across the lines of struggle between urban monarchy and hill-country villages.

Even more important to biblical scholars, this analysis suggests new ways to view the prophets as what Hill calls "local heroes," whose power was rooted in their ability to manipulate Yahwistic language in support of various political factions, and whose roles shifted in the wider context of changes in the national and international political-economic scene.

Thus the task of this cultural textual analysis is to interpret these texts as a historical record of the "lived experience" of a particular people at a specific historical time within the constraints of a particular hegemony, and against the contraints of a particular hegemony. In the case of biblical texts, the historical reconstruction of lived experience is exacting, like piecing together an ancient and intricate weaving, thread by delicate thread. It requires comparative social analysis to understand the structure of power that constrained the lives of the people who told as well as recorded the stories. It also requires a reconstruction of the social history of the period, based on archaeological evidence, analyses of other texts, and the histories of other biblical scholars.

Our analysis also requires the use of historical data from the texts themselves. Needless to say, the reasoning demanded of such intricate tacking back and forth between text and history may at times appear to lead in circles. This is an inevitable hazard of interpretive analysis done at such historical distance with such scanty evidence. Such problems are inherent in even the most informed cultural interpretation. To rephrase the anthropologist Clifford Geertz, the task requires a cultivated ability to "guess at meanings, assess the guesses, and draw explanatory conclusions from the better guesses" (Geertz: 20).

Thus the task of deciphering another culture's meanings, however well-intentioned or organized according to the latest scientific or interpretive paradigms, is a difficult one. And because the subject under investigation is that of religious texts still used in the daily interactions of Judeo-Christian communities, socio-cultural analysis needs as much epistemological integrity as the interpreter can bring to the project. By this I mean that any interpretation is necessarily based on the paradigms that organize the interpreter's own personal and cultural perspective, and is therefore a leap of faith into the historical dark, recognizing that we carry the blinding torch of our own class, cultural, historical, and personal perspectives (cf., e.g., Clifford, Rosaldo).

The Historical Context of the Stories

To place these stories in context, both as examples of a typical anti-monarchic genre and as specific tales from the 9th-century, it is necessary to understand the political-economic and hegemonic constraints that shaped life for various groups of Israelites during this period. The relationship can be conceived as nested boxes, the larger box of Israel in conflict with other Near Eastern states, enclosing and shaping the smaller box of an Israelite monarchy locked in struggle with rural clans.

While the larger interstate context ultimately shaped life for all the Israelites, those who were most directly involved in it, and who wielded power within it, were kings and a handful of urban elites. The interstate struggle of which they were a part created a particular "lived experience" of subordination under the more powerful Near Eastern states, which in turn influenced the way that these elites imposed their dominant hegemony over the Israelite people in the intrastate context. As this dominant hegemony continued to encroach on village life under the Omrids, this created a political atmosphere in which a powerful

Yahwistic, prophet-mediated counter-hegemony, manipulated by a resourceful political faction, could fuel the overthrow of a dynasty.

Israel and the Near East: The Interstate Context

Israel's independent state existence hinged on the absence of the two great Near Eastern powers that clamped themselves around the Palestinian corridor, Egypt and Assyria. Between the mid-12th and 10th centuries B.C.E., a period in which both Assyria and Egypt reduced their influence in the area, Israel evolved from a clan confederation into an agrarian state.

The relationship of Israel to the wider Near Eastern social system is rooted in Israel's evolution as what archaeologists call a "secondary" state in relationship to Egypt and Assyria as "primary" states (Fried: 231). The process began with Egypt and Assyria as they developed independently by establishing modes of production related to their large river systems. Agriculture in these two geographical regions depended on irrigation from these river systems, and provided an opportunity for elaborate, hierarchical political structures to develop out of the control and coordination of the economic system.

As these primary states grew in complexity and extended their military control over surrounding regions, they began to incorporate other groups into their system, either directly or indirectly. The natural expansion route, as well as communication corridor, between the two great states was the area that arched north from the Tigris-Euphrates valley and stretched westward over and around the Arabian desert, plunging south along the Mediterranean coast to Egypt. This is the area where Israel and the rival groups of Phoenicia, Philistia, and the Aramean peoples developed as secondary states, vying with each other for control of crucial trade routes and cities which were temporarily freed from the direct control of Egypt and Assyria (R. Cohen: 39). While Egypt struggled with internal problems, and Assyria busied itself expanding and consolidating in other areas, the small states that occupied this strategic territory were left to fight each other and in the process develop their own state systems.

Under Saul, David, and Solomon Israel managed to wrest out of this disputed territory a narrow corridor of land bounded westward by the sea and eastward by the desert. The two major trade routes connecting Egypt and Assyria came through that corridor on either side of the Jordan and Salt Sea. The most important, the coastal route, ran north to Megiddo in the Jezreel valley, where it branched west along the coast through Tyre and on to what had been Ugarit, and east through Hazor and Damascus. At Damascus it joined routes coming westward from the Euphrates valley and Mesopotamia. The other main route was the King's Highway, which ran through the Transjordanian hill country from the Arabah to Damascus and connected with routes to the Arabian countries and the Red Sea (cf. Aharoni and Avi-Yonah: 9–10; Frank: B15–B16).

These highways linked all the Near Eastern states, and when a major technological development in iron occurred, making it the most important metal in the Near East, these routes became central to major changes in the direction of economics and politics in the entire region.

Through the process called "steeling," iron was made harder than bronze, and therefore more desirable for tools and weapons (Maddin, Muhly, and Wheeler). This technological change triggered a shift in the mode of production throughout the Near East that would profoundly affect the political-economic struggles of the entire region, on international, national, and local levels. For Assyria—a military empire in an agrarian age—a monopoly on the raw material for tools and weapons was imperative to its further expansion in the Near East. Archaeological evidence showing a proliferation of iron implements after 900 B.C.E. indicates that iron productivity had rapidly increased in the region. Iron was now plentifully available for tools as well as weapons and was used, at least by the Assyrians and Babylonians, for axes and hoes as well as furniture and lamps (Ibid.). Obviously, the society that controlled iron trade would monopolize access to the most important tools of production and would therefore dominate the Near East economically as well as militarily. It was clear that Assyria could no longer afford to let the Aramean states retain their independent and uncooperative hegemony over these vital trade routes.

Accordingly, in 884 B.C.E., Asshur-nasir-pal II seized control of the Assyrian empire and marched west to subordinate the Aramean states. By this time, Israel was separate from Judah, and it was probably in that same year, in response to the Assyrian threat, that Omri was able to wrest the government of Israel in a military coup d'état and shift the state's political course from Jeroboam-style isolationism to an outgoing internationalism (Chaney, 1982). Assyria's westward expansion undoubtedly encouraged political factions in Israel to support a military leader who promised to strengthen the state and ensure its survival in the upcoming international struggles.

At least in terms of the state's future as a monarchy, Omri was the appropriate leader. His dynasty thrived for over forty years. However, the price of his international and dynastic success was the complete alienation of several groups of his subjects. One of the key factors causing this was a foreign policy that emphasized the king and his faction's prosperity over a concern for the prosperity of the rest of the country.

Omri pursued those economic interests in the shadow of increased Assyrian aggression, for Assur-nasir-pal II made a second westward campaign to the Mediterranean coast and demanded tribute from Tyre. Meanwhile, the small western states continued to negotiate or war amongst themselves over their respective shares in the booming western Asian economy. Omri began his bid for Israel's share by forming a strong alliance with the maritime societies of Phoenicia, just as Solomon had reportedly done.

The alliance proved symbiotic. The Phoenician economy depended on commerce rather than agriculture (Lenski: 91–92), hence it had to import food, particularly from nearby Israel. Phoenicia also secured access to markets and trade routes going through Israel and into areas not accessible by sea. In turn, Israel benefited from the alliance by selling its agricultural surplus to Phoenicia and gaining access to its international overseas and overland trade routes. Furthermore, Israel's upper classes were able to avail themselves of exotic luxury items and military equipment through Phoenician contacts. The alliance was sealed diplomatically when Omri arranged the marriage of his son Ahab to Jezebel, the daughter of king Ittoba'al of Tyre. Both ruling families profited from their economic relationship and recognized its strategic importance as a balance to the growing ascendancy of Aramean Damascus under Ben-Hadad.

Under this ambitious king, the Damascus-centered kingdom was emerging as a major power in western Syria and Palestine. Omri acknowledged this threat by maintaining strong alliances with both Phoenicia and Judah. Later, during Ahab's reign, Israel and Damascus met at least twice in battle, once at Samaria, and once at Aphek, a border town where the route from Damascus entered Israel. Israel emerged victorious both times (1 Kings 20). The victory gained Ahab a few trade concessions in Damascus and the return of several cities.

These games of love and war for economic prizes continued among the western kingdoms for many years, undisturbed by the outside world except for rumors of Assyrian aggression. Judah continued to thrive economically, sheltered by alliances with Israel both geographically and politically from the brunt of Aramean bellicosity. Egypt to the south had not ventured far into Palestinian politics since Shishak's forays soon after secession. The Philistine cities along the coast had declined in power, and now interfered with Israel primarily as an ally to Damascus, occasionally provoking battle at one of their border towns.

However, the *status quo* was soon shaken when Shalmaneser III succeeded to the Assyrian throne in 859 and marched purposefully westward in his first year of rule. During this campaign he brought Bit-Adini, the Aramean kingdom on the upper Euphrates, completely under his control (Saggs: 98). His economic motive was clear: domination of northern Syria, southern Anatolia, and Cilicia, the principal source areas for iron and silver (Tadmor: 98).

Now that he controlled the important trade routes along the upper Euphrates to Asia Minor, Shalmaneser posed a direct threat to the western nations. Under this common threat, rivalries were suspended and new alliances forged in a coalition of western kings from as far north as Cilicia in Asia Minor and south to Ammon, and perhaps even Egypt.

The coalition was headed by Ben-Hadad of Damascus, Irhuleni of Hamath (north of Phoenicia), and Ahab of Israel. When Shalmaneser struck westward again into Syria, the combined armies met him at Qarqar on the Orontes river. Although Shalmaneser later claimed victory, it appears by his retreat that he had weighed the cost of continuing his campaign and backed down.

According to the biblical narrative (1 Kings 22), the alliance between Israel and Damascus soon broke down, at least enough for them to resume fighting over strategic border towns. In a battle at Ramoth-Gilead on the King's Highway, Ahab was killed in 852. The dynasty continued under Ahaziah, who died within a year accidently (2 Kings 1) and was succeeded by his brother Jehoram.

The "sins of his fathers" now came to full fruition under Jehoram. The war with Ben-Hadad in Gilead continued, draining the nation of men and money. Moab rebelled against its Israelite overlord, and Jehoram could not get the rebels under control. Within the nation, the pent-up frustrations of various classes and factions who had suffered under the Omrid regime began to build to an explosive point. In 842 a revolt broke out, sparked by a military coup d'état led by the general Jehu, who claimed the support of a Yahwistic faction under the prophet Elisha.

The Monarchy and the Yahwists: the Intrastate Context

The stresses experienced by various groups under the Omrids that eventually led to the Jehu revolt can be understood by mapping out first geographic and then political terrains. In contrast to Judah, Israel was crisscrossed with hills that divided many small regions from each other making communication difficult between villages and towns. Even more important perhaps, agriculture depended on rainfall and springs; hence, production was decentralized. Thus, in contrast to countries like Egypt or the Mesopotamian states where river-based agriculture allowed leaders to centralize production and political control, any leader attempting political centralization in Israel had to create a political, economic, and ideological system capable of overcoming the isolation and independence of villages. These villages remained nestled in the hill-country regions, defending their political, economic, and cultural independence and only begrudgingly maintaining tenuous relationships with whatever leader managed to wrest control of the central government.

Israel had a "tribal" tradition of independence from state power that had helped justify the split from the house of David in the first place. After Solomon's death, Israel's elders, fed up with bearing the major burden of economic support and corvée labor for the kingdom, decided to break away from the Davidic state.

After this split, Judah and Israel resumed their developments as separate states and peoples with distinct historical experiences. In the south the Davidic dynasty was established, which endured almost 400 years, while the north rippled with recurrent political factionalism and coups d'état for the remaining 200 years of its history.

For the first 50 years after secession in Israel, village and regional independence thwarted any one group's ability to consolidate power and establish a centralized monarchy. The capital and cult sites changed several times, probably in attempts to appease sectional and regional interests. Kings were unable to balance factions and establish a dynasty. Without such political stability, they could not create an efficient bureaucratic system to exploit the country's land and labor. Villages were therefore freer to pursue their independent interests, unhampered by excessive tax, corvée, and military obligations.

This regional independence came to a halt when Omri's military faction took advantage of the impending threat of Assyrian aggression and managed to win enough support to install Omri as king. Once ensconced on the throne, Omri was compelled to consolidate his power among the tribal villages and push his claims to their land, labor, and crops.

The conflict that ensued after Omri's rise to power had two main fronts. One was between Omri's ruling family and the other elite families who were not directly affiliated with him. This was a conflict within one class for control of that class. The other conflict was between classes, that is, between all the elites and all the peasants who supplied the labor that sustained the social stratification of the system. Actions that Omri and his successors took had effects on both classes, and caused resentment in both classes—which is why disgruntled elites were eventually able to enlist peasant support in a broad-based revolt against the Omrids.[4]

One of the first things Omri did to consolidate his control was to purchase a centrally located piece of land (and possibly existing buildings) at Samaria, a central location not controlled by the established elite clans of Shechem and Tirzah. Here he built his own royal complex and created a bureaucracy of officials and retainers.[5] In order to maintain these underlings' loyalty, he had to remunerate them generously with land, lucrative offices, and political policies all of which would enhance their wealth and prestige. His ability to reward his followers depended on the alliance with Phoenicia, which secured a new source of wealth and luxury items. Since these goods were obtained by trading Israelite-grown foodstuffs, the Israelite governing class looked eagerly for ways to increase the production of easily exportable grains, wine, and oil.

Grains were efficiently grown in the valleys and plain areas like Esdraelon and Sharon, where the land was owned by elites who benefited from the new system. However, vineyards and olive orchards were better suited for the terraced hill areas where villagers had been intercropping for subsistence over generations (Chaney, 1982: 12–16). The elites began devising ways to bring that village land into the agrarian commercialized system. One way, as Todd (Chapter 1 above) suggests, was through a process much like rent capitalism,[6] which enabled elites to

---

[4] Of course, the process was more complex than a simple two-front struggle. There may have been other groups that had their own particular reasons for overturning the Omrids, for example, Jehu makes an overture to Jehonadab, son of Recheb, to "see his zeal for the Lord" on his way to Samaria to kill Ahab's family (2 Kgs 10:15–16). For Samaria, see Stager (1990).

[5] Napier suggests that the Omrids lived in Jezreel and used Samaria as a summer home or royal security refuge. This would not change the essential argument here. The Omrids were still trying to centralize control over the economy, wherever they lived on a permanent basis. If, as Napier indicates, it was the post-Jehu kings who actually presided there full-time, the anti-Samarian rhetoric of the stories at the later written levels may reflect the continued resentment toward the ongoing centralization after the Jehu revolt

[6] The use of the term "rent capitalism," which Todd adopted from others, is problematic, particularly since "capitalism" itself did not evolve as a social system or mode of production until over two millenia later. However, it is likely that this same type of process was used to force peasants off their lands even in pre-capitalist states.

control access to water, work animals, and iron tools by selling or renting at prices which forced the peasants into debt or to sell their land.

There were other, less direct means. The elites could increase the corvée demand on the peasants for building palaces and fortresses to support the lifestyles and military defense of the wealthy. Peasants absent too long from their plots at home would lose their crops, making them susceptible to losing their land to pay taxes and debts owed to elites. Furthermore, the wealthier landowners of the plains, whose fertile soils showed higher productivity than the hill-country plots, could lend money to the peasants and thereby push them into debt.

While scheming to control the hill-country lands, the Omrid kings had to balance their own interests against those of the rest of the governing class. To succeed, they had to keep the other elites dependent on their particular regime and its policies. The trade-off was, in Lenski's terms, between minimizing "the rate of internal political change" and maximizing "production and the resources on which production depends" (Lenski: 41–42). The Omrid productive strategies afforded great opportunities for the upper class to gain power by making money through estate enlargement and trade. To counter this, the king's party tried to keep both land and trade under its direct hegemony. Land could be controlled by keeping much of it in prebendal domain, where the king could offer a particular estate as a reward, or as payment for a particular office. Once it slipped into patrimonial domain, however, it passed down through the landowner's family and the king lost control over it except through taxation (Ibid.: 231ff.). He could only make up for such losses by obtaining more land either through war and other types of legal or illegal acquisition.

As many have suggested, the Naboth story (1 Kgs 21) may generically reflect an illegal transaction of this kind. According to Todd, the story circulated among certain anti-Omrid elite factions, perhaps those that identified most closely with Yahwistic traditions, illustrating how their right of inheritance to land was jeopardized by the king's schemes to keep land in his own hands (Chaney, 1982). It is significant that the estate that Ahab coveted was located in Jezreel,[7] a town near the fertile Esdraelon valley. This area was distant from the capital Samaria, but central to the major producing region and close to Megiddo, where the major trade route ran. Perhaps this area was somewhat independent of

---

[7] The text is ambiguous here as to exactly where Naboth's plot of land is located, Samaria or Jezreel (Napier).

Samaria, and more deeply rooted in Yahwistic culture, in which case Ahab may have wanted to undermine the region's autonomy by breaking up patrimonial estates. The fact that Shunem, where the wealthy woman who supported Elisha lived, was located in the same region, is probably not coincidental (2 Kgs 4:8–17).

The Naboth story has additional significance with its casting of Phoenician Jezebel as the villainess. The story slyly places a sulking Ahab under the thumb of a meddling foreign wife who panders to his greedy whims. To those outside the central court of Samaria, Jezebel epitomized everything that was wrong with the Omrid dynasty. It was Ahab's marriage to Jezebel that secured the alliance with Phoenicia and gave his dynasty resources that allowed him to exploit—and alienate—much of the elite class (Todd, Chapter 1 above). Some elites may have resented the fact that they had to go through royal channels in Samaria to gain from the profitable commercial relationship to Tyre. To add insult to injury, the royal family who controlled those channels monopolized both power and prestige and relegated these other elites to second-class, provincial status. This was too much to swallow for proud Israelites whose forebears had broken from Judah to be independent. Resentment festered among these rural elites, exacerbated by an important ideological quarrel with the royal elite.

This ideological quarrel involved opposing concepts about which gods and which ethical-political system should govern Israel. It was generally accepted throughout the Palestinian corridor that the most high god was the one who controlled rain, since rain was the primary source of their water for agriculture. Both Yahweh and other nations' gods are depicted in storm imagery: wind and fire and quaking (e.g., Cross, 1973: 147–94; Coote: 115–20). The high god made the crops grow and was the source of all fertility. However, throughout Israelite history, conflicts occurred over different conceptions of what Yahweh required in exchange for that fertility. Omri, like Solomon before him, imported to Samaria the cults of Ba'al Melqart and Ashera along with his Phoenician wife Jezebel. He allowed these cults to flourish, encouraging them as an alternative to traditional Yahwism. This made political sense since the cult of Baal suited a socially stratified kingdom more than did tribal Yahwism. The word "Baal" itself means "Lord, " and implies a hierarchical relationship of subordination in relationships between gods/elites and the rest of the population. In contrast, popular Yahwism apparently depicted a god who offers not only rainfall and fertility but also justice within a contractual arrangement with the powers that be.

Omri's attempt to secure and legitimize his newly-acquired regime involved establishing an ideology that would justify his kingship and challenge the Yahwism that for years had kept Israel from forming a strong state apart from the Davidids. He had to convince his rivals that his gods were the most appropriate for their own welfare.

Lenski argues that any political regime that secures a state through violence must eventually legitimate itself through ideology. He calls this the shift from "might" to "right," or from violence to the rule of law (Lenski: 59). For the rule of law to succeed, however, the ruling regime must convince the influential members of the population that this king is in power because he has a commission from the gods to rule this particular country and to bring its subjects prosperity. Therefore, lawgiving had to be accompanied by historical sanction which connected the ruler with a divinely-blessed ancestry, or by religious festivals and fanfare. The tools of convincing included monumental architecture, designed to impress fellow elites and to persuade peasant belief in the power of the ruler and the futility of resistance(Harris: 388; Whitelam, 1986, 1989).

In Israel, as Todd points out, a king had to legitimate himself in terms of the Yahwistic tradition that required a king to exhibit charismatic qualities rather than royal ancestry, including evidence that he was touched by a divine anointing. The mediator of that divine anointing was the prophet who represented himself as the champion of traditional Yahwism. Furthermore, it is likely that a prophet gained credibility through the spread of stories about him and his followers. These stories were fueled by political factions or clans supporting their own political claims; the group that could attach its reputation to a powerful prophet was more likely to win popular support for a claim to the monarchy.

The Omrids defied this Yahwistic tradition, lifting their family beyond the reach of political struggles of the clans by making outside alliances. In deliberate contrast to this strategy, Jehu gained power by playing the Yahwistic power game. He allied himself with the prophet Elisha, who evidently had a large following. Elisha may have also been popularly associated with the prophet Elijah, who was widely considered a true defender of Yahwism. Once in power, Jehu legitimized himself further by having stories about both these figures collected and arranged in a way that claimed all Yahwistic authority for his own regime.

Jehu collected two different kinds of stories, one of which depicted the prophets championing and challenging kings, armies, and elites, and the other portraying prophets interacting with peasants and women who suffered under the Omrids. He probably included stories about the prophets with fellow elites, both rivals and allies—not to mention himself—in an attempt to legitimize his triumphant coup over other clans within Yahwistic terms. The fact that he included stories about subordinate groups like peasants and women indicates that both groups may have played a large part in supporting his revolt.

Since one of the groups represented in these stories appears to be peasants, and all of the women in the stories except one appear to be peasants as well, it will be useful to understand the social position of peasants in Israel, and the pressures placed on their lives by both the foreign and domestic policies of the Omrids.

As pointed out by Todd, the majority of the population in the territory, as in any agrarian society, were peasants (Lenski: 266). Peasants are rural cultivators who are persuaded or coerced to give up much of their produce, money, and labor to a dominant class. Members of the dominant class use these "surpluses" to support their own standard of living and to support other groups in the society, such as artisans, retainers and priests, who do not farm but require payment for their goods and services (Wolf: 1–4,9; Harris: 266–78).

This asymmetrical relationship between peasants and ruling classes in Israel had grown out of centuries of struggle betweeen quasi-independent clans who scratched out a living in the hills, and lowland elites who tried to bring these villages under their control. Within the village systems, individual Israelite families and clans had more control over access to land and other basic resources. If they could maintain relative independence, they could limit the amount of tax, corvée labor, and military service required by a state. Under the Omrid dynasty peasant exploitation was presumably worse then it had been even under the Solomonic united kingdom, because "on a smaller land, resource, and population base than that controlled by Solomon" Ahab supported an even more expensive army, and an equally lavish lifestyle (Chaney, 1982: 15).

There is both archaeological and historical evidence that the Omrids were extravagant in both their military and luxury expenditures. For the battle with Assyria at the Orontes, Ahab amassed a huge army of 2,000 chariots and 10,000 foot soldiers, as recorded in Shalmaneser's annals (Bright: 239). The historical record also indicates that the Omrids built up northern towns along the coastal highway. Excavations at both Hazor and Megiddo have revealed elaborate siege fortifications, including underground water tunnels, which were probably built during this period (Ibid.: 249). Furthermore, archaeological evidence indicates that the Omrids also spent lavishly on their capital city Samaria with its beautiful architectural craftsmanship and huge palace complex (Ibid.: 240). These state projects would have required an enormous amount of taxation and peasant labor, and the social system the Omrids fostered was designed to maximize such exploitation.

This system allowed agrarian elites to live off the peasants' labor parasitically with no means for safeguarding the well-being or survival of those whom it exploited. This was not merely a siphoning off of a "surplus" above and beyond the minimum to sustain the lives of peasants. Most peasant populations do not receive the minimum amount of calories needed "to balance the expenditure of energy a man [or woman] incurs in [their] daily output of labor" (Wolf: 5–6). Nor do they have enough food to provide for next year's crop and the maintenance of their animals and equipment. Yet, although both a caloric minimum and a "replacement fund" are necessary to sustain peasant life, in agrarian states where population increases continued to pressure resources, the elites who directed the society's production and redistribution strategies were not concerned with policies that would sustain all the members of the society. As long as there were enough able bodies to maintain its lifestyle demands, the governing class did not concern itself with those who labored to sustain them.

Exploitation took another form in that the governing class continued to demand increasing surpluses. When peasants with their traditional methods of farming and redistribution did not cooperate, the dominant class sought to change these methods and to control the land themselves. The new commercial opportunities of the Omrid dynasty allowed the upper classes, including the king, to try numerous methods to usurp peasants' land and convert it into cash-crop estates. This created a vicious cycle for peasant cultivators, who could not make ends meet and had to borrow to cover their families' subsistence. Since the chances for repayment were limited, lenders charged increasingly higher interest rates.

Peasants' difficulties increased during times of political instability when kings and elites wrestled for control of the state and its resources. Land changed hands frequently as the king alternately awarded and repossessed the prebendal estates in his political maneuvering. Landowners, uncertain about their tenure, pushed to maximize extracted surplus while in control of a particular piece of land (cf. Wolf: 56; Harris: 302).

Pressures on Israelite peasants increased throughout Ahab's 20 year reign and into the reigns of Ahaziah and Jehoram. Israel was on the downward swing of what Marvin Harris (10–12) calls the "adaptational cycle," moving from expansion of production to depletion of resources with no sign that elites intended to heed negative feedback processes by changing their productive strategies. Ahab had stepped up warfare with Aram and Assyria, to add or retain land and trade resources. But although he was somewhat successful, it made no difference to conditions at home except to burden the peasants with more taxation and corvée to keep up the army and defense building. Even when a severe drought hit Palestine during Ahab's reign the king, according to 1 Kings 18, worried about food for his horses, oblivious that the peasant masses were starving.

So, while the Omrids' centralizing continued to alienate regional elite families, the peasants were being driven to despair and potential violence by latifundialization, warfare, and drought. Their means of subsistence was being destroyed by the governing class and by nature, and as they were forced out of their lands and their families, their social system of clan and village mutual dependence was being torn apart. Their mode of production and the entire way of life that it encompassed were being changed by Omrid politics and the development of centralized state power. The intricate warp and woof of their "lived experience" as a particular kind of people was being pulled apart, thread by cultural thread. Conditions strained toward rebellion, and the discontented rural elites must have been eager to take advantage of the political resource of peasant despair and outrage to overthrow the Omrid regime and install their own leader.[8]

The Stories of Elijah and Elisha as Evidence of Life in Omrid Israel

As mentioned at the outset, within the two cycles of stories featuring Elijah and Elisha, both probably recorded after the Jehu revolution, there are two types of stories, each of which reflects the concerns and experiences of a different class of people in Omrid Israel. The written type of story, replete with historical data and descriptions of interactions between the prophet and kings, army captains, landowners, and other elites, reflects the experiences of the elite. These derive from those

---

[8] Moore (459–74) discusses this kind of elite use of peasants within the capitalist system. I am assuming it is applicable here as well.

regional elites who were marginalized by the Omrid monopoly of prestige and power.⁹

While this first type of story often includes supernatural events and shows some structural similarities to the other stories, these elements are difficult to untangle from the complex political and theological purposes of later editions. This is not surprising, since, following the revolt, elites probably began doctoring these pre-revolt stories to fit their new status of power. Examples of these stories include the Naboth incident (1 Kgs 21); the Baal showdown (1 Kgs 18: 17–46); water supplied for the army (2 Kgs 3:4–17, 20); and the woman's land rights restored (2 Kgs 8:1–6).

In contrast, the second type of oral story shows a distinct lack of broad political awareness. These are the stories that have often baffled biblical scholars and exegetes with their apparent focus on a supernatural event and their lack of moral or theological intention (cf., e.g., Gray: 479 and passim; Montgomery: 39–41; Rofé, 1970: 431). They tend to involve one interaction between a prophet and an individual or a group that has immediate life-and-death concerns.

The following discussion demonstrates how this interaction between characters in the stories gives clues to the lives of everyday Israelites and the ways in which they may have related to prophets. It will also discuss how these descriptions of miraculous interchanges may have served as (1) an oral genre of political warfare between factions and clans throughout northern Israelite history and (2) as specific stories that fueled broad-based support for the anti-Omrid Jehu faction that claimed Elijah and Elisha as their patron prophets.

Thus I argue that an analysis of the relationship between the prophet and the other main character in each story is the first step in unpacking their meaning, rather than a focus on the stories' "supernatural" elements. Scholars often dismiss these tales because of such "magical" overtones, which seem to have no purpose other than to amuse superstitious followers. Both Gray (379, 466) and Montgomery (39–41) typify this approach with their suggestions that these stories belonged to small groups or schools of religious mystics who preserved them for their own

---

⁹ This division corresponds with Gray's classification of the Elisha stories into two similar categories or "sources." The first include those in which Elisha plays a "credible" role in historical events, "usually reflecting the attitude of the conservative party in Israel towards the monarchy...." This part appears similar to what I call the alienated rural elites. The second group are those in which Elisha is more directly involved, usually through a miracle. This group appears to correspond to what I call peasant miracle stories; see Gray, 465.

edification. Such interpretations ignore the possibility that the stories had a broader social significance. Even Wilson (195–206), who investigates the Elijah and Elisha material for clues to the prophetic role in society, neglects these miracle stories as sources for his investigation.

We western scholars are often tripped up in our interpretations of miraculous stories by our ethnocentric and historic limitations. The notion of "miracle" or the "supernatural" is a post-enlightenment Western preoccupation, a result of our conceptual categories of natural vs. supernatural. By contrast, in *these* tales the miracle is a manifestation of power recognized as only one means of problem-solving among many possibilities, including, for example, the help of other people. What is most important in these stories is not the empirical nature of the prophetic powers, but the interaction between the prophet who offers his mediating skills and the people in need of a better connection with the powers that provide health, food, and reproduction.

It is this interaction between the miracle-working prophet and the person receiving the miracle that forms the core of interest in the story, not the "supernatural" event itself. These stories were told and retold because they spread the news of a prophet who helps those who have no other resources to find their own solutions to their seemingly insurmountable problems. The "miracle" in these stories, therefore, does not have to do so much with what we would identify as a marvel that defies scientific notions of cause and effect, but rather the miracle of transformation that the central characters undergo. They begin as individuals resigned to a particular unbearable situation. They become, through the mediation of the prophet, their own liberators from poverty and resignation.

However, it is necessary to understand that while the stories may reflect actual interactions between particular individuals and a prophet, they cannot be fully understood unless these individuals are seen as generic characters, representatives of sub-groups of people within Omrid society who suffered similar hardships and found solutions through a relationship to the prophet. In order to understand this relationship between prophet and marginalized people more thoroughly, it will be helpful to examine briefly the nature of peasant religion in contrast to state religion. Peasant religion centers primarily around the household, the economic and social base of peasant life. These individual households, which may include some configurations of extended family, typically produce what is necessary for their own consumption. They also try to produce whatever is necessary to cover next year's production, the community ceremonial fund, and whatever the overlord and state require from them. Family units often have their own household deities or saints, whom family members tend and petition for favors.

Villages also have their patron gods or saints, who provide a focal point for community ritual and thus mediate tensions between independent households (Wolf: 11 and passim) and provide a common supernatural resource in times of village crisis (Hill, Chapter 2 above). Glimpses of these two kinds of domestic and village religious practices in ancient Israel may be seen in Genesis, where Rachel steals her father's household gods (Gen 31:19), and in Judges, where various tribes celebrate around their local cult locations for Yahweh (as in Shechem in 9:26–28 and Bethel in 21:4).

Both household and village religious practices center around experiences such as birth, death, crop survival, weather conditions, and social relationships (Wolf: 10). Rituals to insure the favor of the gods are carefully followed and preserved. This relationship between peasant and deity resembles the relationship between peasant and earthly authority figure: one must indulge, placate, and carefully petition them both to get what one wants. Thus religion does not provide an abstract system of evil and good, but rather a means to make sure that children remain healthy, grain crops yield abundantly, neighbors do not mistreat you, and drought does not devastate your village.

When disasters occur, the individual or community bargains with deities with renewed intensity. New tactics may be tried. Then, if the prayers are answered, the petitioners feel triumphant in their valiant and intelligent efforts to secure the desired end from their supernatural power source. Peasants tell stories about these events, shaping the narrative to celebrate their own ability to make "a marvelous breakthough in the struggle against oppressive restrictions on human life" by juxtaposing an oppressive context and an extraordinary breaking out of it (Wire, 1978).

I have read transcriptions of such miracle stories told by Mexican immigrant peasants, and solicited some myself in informal fieldwork (E. Miller; Rentería). When using first person, the narrators shaped the story to show how resourceful and courageous they, the tellers, had been in pursuit of a miracle from a particular saint. The story worked rhetorically to convince hearers not only of this particular saint's power over sickness, drought, accidents, and other misfortunes, but also of the wisdom of the person who had struggled to maintain a relationship with a saint and thereby benefited. Furthermore, stories told in the third person had the same structure of intention, as though the teller—although the miracle had not affected him or her directly—wanted the hearer to believe in the saint's power as well as the intelligence of the person who had had the courage and wisdom to choose this particular saint to do a miracle.

Such miracle stories, like those I have witnessed and those recorded in the Bible, appear to celebrate the successful psychological transformation of the social actor who petitions the miracle, moving from despair/skepticism/resignation to triumph over a seemingly insurmountable problem. The point of the stories seems to be not the miracle, but a shift in the main character's sense of the possible which the narrator wants to share with the audience. In fact, stories told by more "sophisticated" peasant immigrants when asked by me for a miracle story, had this same narrative structure of triumph over the difficulties of poverty in Mexico. While they tended to downplay the element of the supernatural, or to question it, their narratives promoted their own triumphs over insurmountable odds with the assistance of some person or saint.

While it is difficult, without further research, to make strong claims about a cross-cultural genre of "miracle," or "transformation" tale, such informal comparisons can suggest new ways to view the biblical stories. It may be that people in positions of powerlessness, like peasants from rural 20th-century Mexico or peasants in 9th-century B.C.E. Israel, may seek relationships with figures like saints or prophets—either actual living figures or representations of those figures—who represent for them untapped sources within themselves of psychological strength with which they may break out of an oppressive context.[10]

This oppressive context of the peasant's life—or of the life of anyone who has little power over their environment—has to do with being dependent on the whims of both nature and authorities. Such vulnerability to nature and authority shows starkly in the simple narratives told by peasants and other powerless people in the Elijah and Elisha miracle stories. These tales emerged under extreme conditions of change, probably originating as first-person stories told by people whose lives had been touched by their interactions with some prophetic figure. They were then probably passed on by family-members and friends, some eventually

---

[10] A Jungian notion of psychological transformation through an encounter with a person/figure that represents the Self might be pursued here. Another idea worth pursuing would be how narrative may play a key role in psychological transformation, a notion suggested by Noel.

becoming adopted into a particular clan's promotion of a prophetic figure in a bid for political power.

The possibility that these stories were reproduced within political struggles between clans is supported by the narrative form of the Elijah and Elisha stories. Most of them describe a single interaction between either an individual or group and one of these prophets. They are told in a report style, like a newspaper story, depicting events as they actually happened. Each story usually gives specific place and time and focuses on short action scenes. Characterization is suggested through action, the point of view is usually third person, and words and phrases are carefully chosen to enhance the sense that it is a true story (Wire, 1981).

Furthermore, unlike a report, this story type exhibits exhortative features, encouraging the hearer to believe that, contrary to the onerous status quo, significant changes can be made in desperate lives. The plot moves forward quickly, creating tension and drama by running the ultimately triumphant narrative against an implicit anti-narrative of despair and resignation.[11] The teller behind the story depicts a powerful prophet who can solve the problems of destitute people. The purpose of telling the story is the story's triumph. Listeners are encouraged to believe that prophets, and this prophet in particular, not only care about the problems of widows, the poor, debtors, and the homeless, but can also do something about them.

Wire (1978: 86) suggests that the structural tensions within the miracle stories can be isolated from the literary context to give access, not necessarily to the oral original, but to the essential meaning of once telling the story orally—that is, its intention within an interaction between a teller and a hearer. The interaction between characters in this story mirrors the teller's purpose and is the "constructive, hence interpretive key" (Ibid.: 83).

Thus, the structure of the interaction between prophet and person is a key to the purpose of the story as a type of propoganda for the prophet. However, characterization is also key to understanding the stories' origin and purpose. The characters who interact with Elijah or Elisha in these stories include men who are primarily his followers, or the "guild prophets," and women whom he encounters on his journeys around the countryside, as well as a few anonymous clusters of people. All of the characters with whom the prophet interacts have some basic, usually

---

[11] I have borrowed the idea of anti-narrative from Wire (1981) and extended it to create brief anti-narratives for each story.

desperate need for help. While we have no direct knowledge of what daily life must have entailed for the people that these stories describe, an analysis of each story in terms of both structure and content, within the wider context of the previous comparative historical reconstruction, may yield clues about (1) life for the least powerful in Omrid Israel, (2) the role of the prophet in ancient Israel, and (3) the nature of these stories and the reason they were included in the national literature.

Elijah and the Poor Widow: I Kings 17:8–24

The first story is that of Elijah and the widow, a two-part story that develops the relationship of the prophet to a poor woman. In the first part of the story, we see the prophet confronting the woman and initiating a relationship with her by making a demand. In the second part, the woman, who now apparently keeps a room for Elijah, confronts the prophet and makes a demand in exchange. The transactional relationship between them is a clue both to how women followers may have related to the prophets, and to how the story itself is a kind of advertisement for belief in the prophet's ability to provide solutions to problems.

In the first part, the prophet meets a woman gathering sticks at the city gate. Already there is an indication that this woman is not wealthy. If she were, she would not be at the outskirts of the city collecting her own kindling. The prophet Elijah confronts her by asking for water. Without a word in response, she turns to get it for him, as though following orders from demanding superiors is something to which she is accustomed. But he still does not let her go, pushing her further to interact with him by requesting a piece of bread. Now she responds to him with an oath that seems like a challenge: "As Yahweh your god lives, would that I could bake cakes; there is only a handful of flour in my jar and a little oil in my jug." She then explains that she is about to prepare a last meal for herself and her son, and then resign herself to die.

The prophet still does not back off from his request. He meets her objections with authority, telling her not to be afraid, but to fix a cake and bring it to him. Then, after she has taken care of him, the prophet says she will be able to feed herself and her son. This, he assures her, is by the authority of Yahweh, the god of Israel who has promised that the supply of flour and oil will not run out until he makes it rain again. She then stops resisting him, and in v. 15 goes to do as Elijah has directed.

Tension is built within this first section of the narrative through Elijah's requests and the woman's resigned objections. The resolution, however, does not revolve around the supernatural provision of oil and meal. Rather, tension is resolved between the two characters when the woman surrenders her negative attitude and goes to carry out Elijah's instructions. The denouement and purpose of this section of the story are designed to convince the woman to believe that this prophet has the power to help her provide for herself. The key here is that *he* does not do the miracle *for her*, but enables her to do it *for herself*. Just as importantly, he does not pretend to be doing the favor without any strings attached. He requests her to feed him as a preliminary gesture to being able to feed herself. Thus the relationship between them is transactional: he will empower her, and she will feed him.

The conflict between Elijah's charismatic power and the widow's apathy creates the rhetorical tension between the narrator and the reader, or perhaps a clan storyteller and her audience. The story engages the reader, or hearer, in a power struggle not only between characters in the story, but between the teller and the reader/hearer herself. This is campaign rhetoric of a sort. One can imagine the oral teller of this story performing in order to convince people who, like this widow, had been victimized by the harsh conditions of famine and the structural inequalities of the monarchic system. People like this probably felt powerless to change the desperate conditions under which they lived. The prophet's power provided an alternative to despair. The teller would be sensitive to the audience's concerns and would pit their implicit story of resignation and poverty against this story of power and plenty.

The audience's experience and subjective attitude toward that experience provides the anti-narrative against which the storyteller's narrative must struggle and win. This anti-narrative can be read between the lines, using some historical conjecture and knowledge about Israel during the 9th century. This is the context that can be indirectly inferred through the details and the structural intention of the text. The anti-narrative might look like this if it were explicitly told:

> There were many widows in Omrid Israel and the surrounding areas because of war and famine. Traditional family and village systems of support for widows had broken down since the king and his elites had started buying up the land and corrupting village leaders. Prices for oil and meal were high because they were chief export crops. This widow could not afford them anymore. She cooked one last meal for herself and her son and they both died soon after.

People for whom this anti-narrative was a familiar experience would hear the story of Elijah and the widow and would look to the prophet for a similar solution to their own desperate situations.

In the second half of the story, it appears that Elijah has become a regular guest in the house of this woman since he is staying in an upper room (v. 19). The son of the woman becomes ill and stops breathing. His mother, who has been sheltering Elijah, turns on the prophet angrily, asking him accusingly, "What is there in common between you and me, man of gods?" The question pushes Elijah to define just what their agreement *is*, that is, what the transactional partnership involves if his presence in her house has not kept her son from becoming ill. In fact, she even goes so far as to accuse the prophet of killing her son.

This dramatic accusation and demand force Elijah to act and to keep his part of the bargain with one of his supporters. The woman's question raises the question for the Israelite hearers of the story as well: does Elijah really have an inside track to the gods? The teller draws them toward the answer as the narration takes Elijah up the stairs where he places the boy on his bed and turns to Yahweh. Now it is the prophet's turn to question *his* patron angrily. He asks him why he should choose this woman to afflict. The teller shows how the prophet struggles to bring his follower's demand to the higher authority. His dramatic gesture—which may have some unknown cultural significance beyond its dramatic effectiveness—of stretching himself out upon the child three times and calling out to the Lord (v. 21) works to build tension: Is this a man of God or an ineffectual, posturing fake? His authenticity as a representative of God becomes apparent to the hearer when the child revives. The story continues to resolve itself, however, beyond the actual miracle, as Elijah walks down the stairs and presents the cured son to his mother. This face-to-face contact between prophet and petitioner confirms that the bargain has been kept, and the woman's loyalty rewarded.

The anti-narrative of this second part of the story indicates that Israelite hearers of the story may have been familiar with prophets who took advantage of followers and did not provide for them as promised:

> Prophets of all sorts abounded in Israel, and you had to be careful about which ones you could trust to truly protect you. A poor widow woman sheltered a prophet in her home, and although he provided food for her, her son died. Women had become accustomed to losing children, since so many children died in Israelite villages due to famine and the resulting spread of disease by people migrating in search of work and

food. The fact that the prophet could not help her proved that he was not really a man of God but only a charlatan whose presence had brought down the wrath of God and killed her son.

The successful resolution of this story declares to those hearing it, or reading it, that this prophet Elijah is the real thing—a genuinely powerful intermediary between poor widows and the god he claims to represent, Yahweh, "the Lord, the God of Israel" (v. 14).

Elisha and the Shunammite Patroness: 2 Kings 4: 8-17

In the next story, the woman depicted is not poor, nor is she a widow; however, she feeds and shelters the prophet and allows him to solve a problem that she shares with all Israelite women, regardless of their social class. The woman in the story is a "woman of influence," hence probably not a poor peasant. She lives in Shunem, on the edge of the Jezreel valley and out of the direct reach of the royal capital Samaria. It appears that her husband is a grain farmer since the word translated "reapers" is associated with grain-binding (Gray: 498). She is probably a wealthy peasant, or a member of the latifundial upper class in the Esdraelon Valley area associated with Jezreel and with the Jehu revolt. However, the story does not indicate that the woman is particularly concerned with larger political issues. Like the woman in the earlier story, she has her own personal reasons for associating with the prophet.

The story, like the earlier one, has a two-part structure in which the relationship between the prophet and the woman develops transactionally. The first part of the story's structure involves an interaction between the woman and Elisha, with Gehazi, Elisha's servant, serving a minor role as intermediary. In the first scene, the woman initiates the relationship with the prophet, first by urging him to dine with her (v. 8) and then by having her husband add on a room for him. At this point, it is not apparent why such a woman would want to befriend a prophet. Perhaps she is trying to secure a useful ally, or sponsor a "hero" for her clan, in the way that Hill (Chapter 2 above) suggests.

Then the prophet tries to figure out what he can do in return for her hospitality, and this interaction is what organizes the essential structure of the story. As in the previous story of the widow, the prophet opens the negotiations between them and performs an unsolicited miracle. First, he asks her directly what she wants in return for her hospitality, pressuring her to acknowledge that she has helped him for a reason. He asks if perhaps he can act as a mediator between her and the king, or perhaps between her and the commander of the army. This was a crucial question since Jehu the usurper was an army commander. She responds, however, that she lives among her own people, an indication, perhaps, that her interests are family- or clan-oriented.

Elisha then asks his servant for advice about what he might do for her. The servant's answer is revealing in two distinct ways. As Gehazi indicates to Elisha, the woman needs a son because her husband is elderly (v. 14). On the one hand, in a patriarchal, patrilineal society like that of Israelite villages (Gottwald, 1979: 285–87) a son was needed to pass on the family heritage. The woman may be acting out of family/clan loyalty, concerned that the line not end with her husband.

On the other hand, she may also have another concern as a woman, which need not have been incompatible with the above concern. Her interests as a woman in such a patriarchal society are protected only when she provides a son for the family. A woman without a son, no matter how wealthy, holds only a tentative place in the family of her husband. In such a patrilineal, patrilocal system, a woman leaves her own family to live with her husband's family, and her children belong to her husband's lineage. As an outsider to this household, she has little power or status until she bears children and has grown sons to protect her interests (Niditch, Collier).

Other biblical examples of the plight of the childless Israelite woman are Sarah, Rebecca, and Rachel. Despite the fact that the (probably male) scribe describes her as jealous of her sister, Rachel was not simply being childishly histrionic when she said to her husband, "Give me children or I shall die!" (Gen 30:1). She was undoubtedly petrified by the prospect of the childless woman's fate (cf. Niditch: 144).

In this vein, it is possible to view the levirate law of ancient Israel as a patriarchal threat. By this law, if she had contributed no sons to the family, she could be given to the next male in the clan, preventing her from returning to her own family where she could perhaps have enough leverage amongst its members to arrange for a marriage more suited to her own interests. Thus, while the levirate can be viewed as protecting women from poverty and an insurance that she would be provided with sons and family ties, I subscribe to a more conflict-oriented interpretation of gender relations.[12] This Shunammite, like any intelligent political

---

[12] Although Elisha represented traditional Yahwism, and thus presumably supported the law of the levirate, it is possible that the Shunammite may have been using the prophet for her own purposes, which may be in tension with some of

actor, was looking out for her own interests as a woman when she made a connection with Elisha.

Nevertheless, despite the probability that Gehazi has accurately assessed her needs, the woman continues to resist Elisha's overtures (v. 16). Her opposition is finally overcome, and the first half of the story's tension resolved, when she conceives as the prophet has promised and bears a son.

In this part of the story, dramatic tension leading to this positive resolution results from the opposing movements of narrative against anti-narrative. The anti-narrative for this woman's life, as in so many women's lives, might be similar to the following:

> A woman's husband died, and since she had no children, she was married to a distant male cousin within her husband's family. She was made to leave her home and community to go to live with him, starting all over again as she had as a young bride, with no security, status, or power in a strange household.

The narrative that ran against such an anti-narrative would skillfully draw upper-class women, as well as other women, into the drama of her story, involving them emotionally in a vicarious fight for a positive change in their lives. It would also work to convince them that the prophet was an able ally for women's interests.

In the next part of the story, the Shunnamite is shown in more active pursuit of her own concerns with the prophet. When the son that Elisha has enabled her to bear becomes ill and dies, the woman refuses to accept his death and immediately sets out to demand a favor from the prophet she has been supporting. Opposition to the success of her mission and to

---

Elisha's Yahwism. Men's and women's interests were probably not always the same within Yahwist culture.

Niditch suggests that the levirate "helped society avoid a sociological misfit, the young childless widow." She draws from the anthropologist Mary Douglas' work, suggesting that this kind of "sociological" approach "deals with the stability and health of the Israelite social structure." Harlots and childless women are "outside the social structure," and therefore a law that kept women married would benefit the society. I disagree with the social model underlying Douglas' and Niditch's work. The implication is that society is like an organism that needs to stay in balance in order to stay healthy. I see social structures like agrarian Israel as arenas where conflict and power struggles are the norm. Laws are not enacted to keep societies stable and healthy. They are wrested out of conflicts between factions with varying degrees of power, each group looking out for its own interests. This would include relationships between men and women.

the positive outcome of the story is posed by her husband's questions about why she is leaving to see the prophet even when it is neither the new moon, nor the sabbath, by the long trip, by Gehazi's pushing her away, and by the prophet's reluctance to come personally. The woman's courage and assertiveness against these odds—"As the Lord lives and as you yourself live, I will not release you" (v. 30)—demonstrate her conviction that she has the right to demand the prophet's personal presence to heal her son. Elisha confirms that right, finally, by going with her.

It is significant that the opposition in the story comes from males—her husband, Gehazi, and even the prophet himself. The story is constructed to appeal to a woman's point of view. The Shunammite's husband doesn't understand why she would need to see the holy man on any days but official religious days—"It is neither the new moon nor the Sabbath" (v. 23)—even though he knows that his son had been ill earlier, since it was he who sent him in to his mother with the servant. The storyteller may be using the husband as a device to illustrate the conventional view that holy men are to be used only for religious functions. In contrast, the woman demands an immediate, personal, service, a miracle, from this man with whom she has formed a transactional relationship. The story's point here is that this prophet is different from a simple religious functionary, and that women understand this better than men.

Gehazi's opposition also emphasizes Elisha's uniqueness. Gehazi's move to intervene between the woman and the prophet (v. 27), as well as his ineffectual attempt to serve as the prophet's surrogate in healing the boy (v. 31), highlight the fact that no one, even Elisha's servant, can stand in for this prophet. This may also be an attack by the storyteller, either at the oral or written level, on possible splinter groups claiming to represent Elisha, represented here by Gehazi.

The prophet's reluctance to come with the woman immediately serves above all to heighten the picture of the woman's strength in demanding her rights with the prophet. She has formed a personal relationship with him, and she demands his actual presence for the healing of her son. She is proven right when Gehazi is unable to heal the boy, even with the prophet's staff. Thus, the storyteller skillfully manages to present a scene that depicts two equal partners in a transactional relationship: a strong woman forming a relationship and claiming her rights within it, and a prophet whose power and Yahweh-derived authority cannot be duplicated.

Once at the house, the tension builds as Elisha comes to the dead boy and tries to revive him. His healing powers are highlighted by the dramatic recounting of how he stretches himself over the child, paces the room, and then lies down on the child again (vv.34–35). The story, however, does not resolve itself the moment the son revives, but rather when Elisha returns him to his mother, thus confirming to her and the audience that the prophet can be counted on to keep his obligations to his followers.

The anti-narrative for this story would go something like this:

> A wealthy woman had a son, but he died suddenly. Despairing, not only out of grief, but because her husband was old and might not be able to give her another son, she searched for someone to help her. But her husband told her that there was nothing that anyone could do, since so many children were dying; it must be God's will. She went to a man who claimed to be a prophet, but he couldn't help her, so she resigned herself to a fate without children to help her in her old age, to protect her interests, and to give her standing in the community.

It would also include a description of the large mortality rate in northern Israel due to famine and the resulting spread of disease by people migrating in search of work and food (cf. Thompson and Lewis: 394). Women who lost their children not only grieved, but also lost status in their homes and communities. Prophets probably attracted many such women from both the poorer peasant classes as well as the upper classes for just these reasons.

Elisha and the Guild Prophet's Widow: 2 Kings 4:1-7

In the next story, a widow of one of the "sons of the prophets" faces the loss of her children in a different way. She has inherited her husband's debt, and since she is unable to pay it, the creditor has threatened to take her children as payment. Like the women in the previous stories, she confronts Elisha and challenges him, reminding him that her husband feared Yahweh, undoubtedly a reference to the fact that he was a member of Elisha's close followers, and therefore his widow is entitled to the prophet's care. Elisha responds to her graciously, acknowledging their relationship and his obligation to her by asking what he might do for her. The obstacles to the successful resolution of the problem and the story include the explicit instructions he gives to her regarding the oil vessels and her obedience to these instructions, an elaborate procedure that involves her children borrowing numerous vessels from neighbors, closing the door on themselves, and then working as a team to fill the jars.

Again, the story does not climax with the miracle. It is resolved when the widow returns to Elisha and he tells her to pay off her creditor and live on the oil she has provided for herself by coming to him for help and following his instructions.

The woman's story, or the anti-narrative, was probably a common one amongst villagers of all classes during the Omrid years.

> A peasant woman's husband, no longer able to sustain his family because he had no land and his family was broken up—brothers sent to work on the king's fortifications in Megiddo and Hazor, a father who lost his land from debt—in despair turned to a prophet for spiritual and material guidance. He became one of his closest followers. However, when the man died suddenly, his wife was left with all his debts. She turned to the prophet for help, but he spurned her, saying that she would have to provide for herself. She then had to sell one of her children into debt slavery so that she and the other children could survive.

The story celebrates the husband's wisdom in following this prophet who claimed to represent Yahweh, and in trusting Elisha to help him secure food for himself and his household, thus perhaps freeing himself from debt. When he died still owing money to creditors, the story shows that Elisha kept his obligations to such followers and their families who were in trouble. It also proclaims the widow's courage in pursuing her rights with the prophet. This story could have circulated as an assurance to the women dependents of followers, or potential followers, that Elisha would help them feed themselves and keep their families together.

The next two stories involve Elisha and his guild prophets. These guild prophets, or "sons of the prophets," are men who can probably be understood as what anthropologist Bailey (44–49) calls a "core group," followers tied to a leader through a loyalty that binds them to him on several levels. The relationship may be symbolized by kinship terminology (such as *sons* of the prophets) and be couched in ideological or religious language. Bailey (37–43) characterizes this kind of relationship between a charismatic leader and his unpaid followers as a "moral" transaction, in which the faithful remain loyal to a leader who embodies some ideal for them. Unlike a "mercenary" transaction in which followers expect to be paid, in a "moral" relationship they simply expect to be fed physically and spiritually. "The service is its own reward."

While Bailey's description is a valuable starting point, I believe that he fails to recognize the immediate transactional benefits that followers may reap from loyalty to a charismatic leader like Elijah or Elisha. To be fed spiritually may involve a psychological transaction of empowerment, which may be just as valuable to a follower as being remunerated materially. Although the prophet may perform some ritual action, or give the instructions for his followers to perform one, the point of the stories is that people become empowered by relating to a prophet. The following stories should illustrate just what these core supporters received in return for their loyalty—besides being fed—and what hearers of the stories could expect if they followed the prophet as well.

Elisha, the Guild Prophets, and the Stew: 2 Kings 4: 38-41

In this story Elisha is depicted seated with his "guild prophets" before him, when he instructs his "young retainer" to prepare stew for the entire group (v. 38). One of the men then goes out to scrounge for herbs and returns with a clothful of wild gourds, which he puts in the pot (v. 39). The storyteller creates tension by painting this narrative against the following anti-narrative which probably functioned as a backdrop in his audience's minds:

> The famine drove hungry people to eat whatever they could find. Many people died because they ate unfamiliar poison foods. Their own familiar food, which they had once grown at home on their own lands, was now sold at the market for extravagant prices that they could not afford. People followed prophets who promised them spiritual enlightenment and full stomachs, but they were often fooled by false promises. This group of men, who formed a religious community, got together to make stew, and one of the wild gourds they gathered and put in the pot poisoned them. Some became ill and others died.

The audience's anti-narrative suspicions are confirmed when the guild prophets in the story begin to eat the stew and discover it is poisoned: "Man of God, there is poison in the pot!" (v. 40) Elisha counters his followers' doubts regarding his abilities as a provider by involving them in a miraculous cure of the stew, instructing them to bring him meal to be thrown into the pot.

This magical "instrumental action" (Gottwald, 1976b) of throwing the meal into the pot takes a subordinate role to the narrative's key structural organization (cf. Wire, 1978: 98). It becomes just another type of interaction between prophet and follower in which powerless individuals take action to change their situation. The story shows that Elisha not only feeds his followers, but also enables them to overcome the daily hazards of trying to eat during a famine. Hearers of the tale would be encouraged to believe that through Elisha's mediation as a prophet of Yahweh, people can become empowered in the midst of overwhelming circumstances like famine.

Elisha, the Guild Prophets,
and the Lost Ax: 1 Kings 6: 1–7

Another story that associates Elisha with the sons of the prophets describes an incident in which Elisha helps his followers build shelters for themselves. One of the men asks the prophet to accompany them to the Jordan, where they plan to cut down trees. When one man's iron axhead falls off into the water, he calls on Elisha, crying out that it was borrowed. For a poor man, losing a borrowed iron implement like this would devastate him financially. Iron was probably used primarily by the military, making it scarce for agricultural use and thus costly; furthermore, the tool may have been borrowed from a creditor (Chaney, oral communication). Elisha throws a stick into the water and magically brings the axhead to the surface. The story's tension does not ease until the man who had asked for the prophet's help reaches down and grasps the resurfaced axhead for himself. As in the other stories, the prophet always involves the petitioners in the miracle, enabling them to have power in their lives.

The anti-narrative of this story, familiar to hearers who had suffered similar bad luck, might go like this:

> A member of Elisha's inner circle borrowed an ax from a local wealthy man who wanted to buy his patch of land. While he was using it to cut down trees for a shelter, the iron axhead slipped from its handle and fell into the river nearby. The man had to go back to the lender and turn over his land to him in return for the lost tool, since iron was expensive and he had no money. He went to work afterward as a day laborer, barely able to feed his family.

Elisha, his Right-hand Man,
and Feeding the Crowd: 2 Kings 4: 42-44

This next story, which probably involves Elisha's core followers, revolves around an interaction between Elisha and his "right-hand man."

Elisha tells him to feed a crowd of a hundred with a small amount of food brought to them by an apparently prosperous supporter. The mention of this crowd in this story hints that Elisha attracted large groups of people. We have no way of knowing just what they were coming to Elisha for—perhaps teaching, healing, food, or as members of some clan trying to gain his patronage. He also has well-to-do supporters who send him provisions, something already evidenced by his relationship to the Shunammite in the earlier story.

Elisha uses these provisions as an opportunity to demonstrate once again that he is an ample provider in the midst of famine. However, when he tells his follower to feed the crowd, even this "right-hand-man" resists by objecting that 20 barley loaves and some fresh ears of grain will not feed 100 men. The anti-narrative running through the audience's mind must have included the knowledge that people often went hungry when they went to hear prophets speak. But Elisha, invoking his authority as a representative of Yahweh, insists "Give it to the people to eat.... For thus says the Lord, 'They shall eat and there shall be some left over'" (v. 43).

The story is resolved when the right-hand-man obeys Elisha's instructions, feeds the crowd, and, says the storyteller, "when they had eaten, there was some left over, as the Lord had said." It is significant that unlike the previous story, the supernatural nature of the provision is not even alluded to here. The point of the story, as for all the stories, is empowerment. In this case, Elisha, through the authority of Yahweh, empowers his core followers to feed themselves.

Elisha and the Spring: 2 Kings 2:19-22

The last story of the series describes an interaction between Elisha and the inhabitants of an anonymous city who ask Elisha to purify a polluted spring. The story appears truncated, as if a longer version has been cut off and fitted with the Deuteronomistic formula "to this day." While the story begins with a petition for a solution to a problem, no tension is built within the narrative, and the only interaction occurring between Elisha and the people is his direction to bring him a bowl of salt, which he uses to purify the water. While there is no real struggle here between narrative and anti-narrative, the transaction aspect of the relationship between characters is not lost. Elisha is pictured as a leader who helps people solve their individual as well as collective problems.

This particular collective problem probably occurred often during the famine years. Common water sources like this spring became polluted with infectious diseases due to customary waste disposal and manuring practices. Diseases spread easily through common use of water sources, particularly during times of famine when large groups of people migrated, lived in close quarters, and were malnourished (cf. Thompson and Lewis: 394).

The Stories as Tales of Resistance

While none of these Elijah-Elisha stories expresses explicit anti-Omrid sentiment, they nevertheless can be interpreted as tales of resistance or counter-hegemony. Indeed, their survival as self-contained units of meaning can be viewed as a form of counter-hegemonic expression preserved within the dominant hegemony. In other words, while the literature that ultimately preserved these stories was monarchic, these stories reveal glimpses of "the lived experience of subordination and domination" of people who did not benefit from the monarchic system, and who continued to live according to a cultural reality that implicitly or explicitly challenged the dominant hegemony of an urban-based monarchic Yahwism. Accordingly, the stories defy monarchic reality, both in what they reveal about life in Omrid Israel for certain key groups of people and in what they demonstrate about transactional relationships between these people and traditional Yahwistic prophets.

The following discussion outlines four different aspects of the dynamics of this struggle between disparate Israelite cultural realities. The first concerns the stories' revelations regarding the lived experience of people completely outside of monarchic urban circles. These include high and low-status women as well as men who were probably disenfranchised peasants. The second discusses the stories' clues about prophet-follower relationships and how personal interaction with a Yahwist prophet was an intrinsically anti-monarchic rural cultural practice. The third deals with the role of the Elijah-Elisha stories, and perhaps of Elijah and Elisha themselves, in the struggle between the rural-highland–traditional-village-Yahwistic counter-hegemony versus the urban-lowland–international-monarchic-Baal/Yahwistic hegemony. The fourth concerns how rural Yahwist stories that reflect the experiences of local, village people became incorporated into legitimation narratives about central urban kings and elites.

The Characters in the Stories

The characters who interact with the prophets in these stories include women from several different social strata, and men who appear to be homeless ex-peasants cut off from their former roles in traditional village life.

The overwhelming evidence in these stories concerning women is that they carried the responsibility for the reproduction of families and clans by their bearing and successfully raising children. It is a *biological* fact, of course, that women must bear children in any society, if they are to be born at all; however, it is a *cultural* fact that women in ancient Israel were apparently expected (1) to bear children in order to insure the reproduction of the family/clan and secure their own place in that family/clan, as in the Shunammite story (2 Kgs 4:8–17); (2) feed those children even when they had no support from family, as in the poor widow and cakes story (1 Kgs 17: 8–24) and the guild prophet's widow story (2 Kgs 4:1–7); (3) insure the health of those children, as in the Shunammite story and the poor widow's story. Whether or not these women felt that these roles were natural—loving their children and going to extremes to preserve their lives—these roles were culturally created and part of a larger patriarchal hegemonic shared by the village Yahwistic system and the urban monarchic system. Thus, although women in ancient Israel undoubtedly had many social roles, they were possibly judged as human beings to a large extent in terms of how they performed as mothers, i.e., custodians of the biological reproduction of the clan.

Under the Omrids' corrupt monarchy, women's maternal duties were made more difficult. First, it appears that young widowhood was a common fate, leaving numerous Israelite mothers and their children more vulnerable to famine and economic exploitation than they would have been with the help of their husbands. There were probably many widows in Omrid Israel because both the intrastate and interstate political-economic maneuvers of these monarchs required vast amounts of corvée labor. Men were conscripted from their villages and families to build palaces and fortifications and to serve as foot soldiers in the Omrids' vast armies. Many of them undoubtedly died due to the harsh conditions of their labor.

Second, it appears that women had become familiar with the bitter possibility of losing their children through disease, hunger, or debt slavery. All of these losses can be traced to political-economic conditions created by Omrid policies and the monarchic, agrarian social system.

Disease and hunger undoubtedly had occurred even outside of the monarchic system; however, it is likely that they occurred more often under the Omrids because their policies exploited peasants without concern for their survival. There were no state provisions for drought conditions, i.e., storing food, lowering taxes, or discontinuing corvée demands of peasant cultivators. Disease was spread because of increased migration due to famine and the vulnerability of hungry people to infection. Furthermore, debt like that experienced by the guild prophet's widow was probably a recent intrusion into village economic life, making widows all that much more vulnerable by burdening them not only with the sustenance of their children, but also with paying for their husband's debts.

The other key group of people characterized in these stories are the male followers of Elisha, which include Gehazi, an anonymous "right-hand-man," and numerous members of the guild prophets. The stories give few clues about the origins of these men; however, they do indicate that they were probably poor. For example, the guild prophet's widow story (2 Kgs 4:1–7) illustrates that some guild prophets were so indebted that upon their deaths, their wives had to consider selling their children. In the Elisha and the lost ax story (2 Kgs 6:1–7) the guild prophet is distressed about losing an ax, one he probably borrowed at considerable risk to his own financial security. In the same story, the guild prophets live in crowded conditions with Elisha and decide to build themselves a shelter; thus it is apparent that none of them is wealthy enough to offer a place for them all to stay, nor do any of them have servants to build them shelter. Furthermore, the poisoned stew story (2 Kgs 4: 38–41) shows the guild prophets relying on the prophet for food, indicating that none of them can supply his own sustenance.

This apparent poverty suggests several different possibilities about the guild prophets' origins. These men may have included people who voluntarily gave up their livelihoods to follow a leader because of an intense Yahwistic religious conviction; however, it was more likely a case of mixed motivation. The group probably included village men who, due to the upheavals of the Omrid period, were no longer able to sustain their lives in traditional village systems. Some may have lost their patrimonial lands to regional elites who were greedy for hill-country lands to grow crops for the international market. They might also have included soldiers returned from serving in Omrid armies who either had no lands to farm, or were seeking alternatives to traditional village life because they had gotten a glimpse of a wider world by moving outside of their villages.

The Prophet in Transactional Relationship

The relationships between the prophet and the men and women with whom he interacts in these stories is a clue to the prophet's role as a resistance figure. For both men and women who interact with him, the transaction empowers them as social actors. For women, this empowerment is within the social arena of the family; for example, the poor widow is enabled to feed her son and save him from death (1 Kgs 17: 8–24); the Shunammite conceives a son, saves him from death, and thus saves her own family standing as well as her husband's (2 Kgs 4: 8–36); and the guild prophet's widow saves her children from debt slavery (2 Kgs 4:1–7). In this way, in a time when the fabric of their social lives is being torn apart by forces they cannot control—nature and a corrupt monarchy—the prophet restores these women to their roles as mothers; and in the case of the Shunammite and the poor widow, he gives them new roles as patronesses of a Yahwistic prophet.

With the men followers, or guild prophets, the social arena is outside the family. It appears that through the prophet they gain (1) power to solve their personal problems, as with the man who lost the borrowed ax (2 Kgs 6:1–7); and (2) power to help other people, as with the followers who are enabled to feed not only each other in the poisoned stew story (2 Kgs 4: 38–41) but also other people in the crowd and the loaves story (2 Kgs 4: 42–44). Thus the prophet gives these men a social role in a time when many village men's roles have been destroyed through social upheaval.

It is this service of the prophet as portrayed in the stories—the prophet as enabler—that provides another sense in which these stories can be conceived as counter-hegemonic. Monarchic power within an agrarian system robbed village and regional people of their collective and individual autonomy. A way of life, a culture, was unraveling as the monarchy increased its hegemony over the hill-country people. Economically, peasants were losing their lands and their livelihoods by latifundialization and increased taxation. Politically, local village and clan relationships were threatened by increasing Omrid interference through centralization. And the very way that northern Israelites conceived of their lives as a unique people—united through an apparent covenant with a god who offered justice within a contractual arrangement—was being stripped from them as the Omrids increasingly tried to co-opt traditional Yahwism.

These stories promote a connection with Elijah and Elisha as an alternative power source for Israelite villagers, a connection that by its very nature defied the state monopoly on Yahwism because this prophet offered a relationship with a local, home-grown, rooted-in-northern-Israelite-hill-country-tradition "hero" as opposed to a relationship with an increasingly remote, bureaucratized, foreign and injust monarch; and because the relationship this prophet offered was transactional, or *contractual*, in the spirit of traditional Yahwism, giving individuals room to negotiate and a sense of their own empowerment. This kind of personal, negotiable relationship with an "authority" figure was profoundly different from the impersonal, distant, and hierarchical relationship offered by a monarch.

The Shunammite woman, the Zarephath widow, and the guild prophet's widow all understand and act on this transactional basis of their relationship to the prophet. The stories describe them demanding that he return their loyalty with help during crisis; but the help is never a hand-out or charity. The prophet acknowledges he needs them as followers by responding to their petition, and he does not elevate himself above them by performing miracles *for* them, but rather helps them to perform the miracles themselves. This is also true of his relationship to his male followers, particularly the sons of the prophets. In the stew story, the crowd-feeding story, and the axhead-recovery story, the powerless individuals who ask for help are rewarded with an empowering instruction to help themselves.

This is not to say that the prophet offered a relationship of total equality. The characters in the stories recognize him as a man with special powers and a unique connection to the supreme diety, Yahweh. For example, the poor widow calls Elijah "Man of God," and the guild prophet in the ax story calls Elisha, "Master!" But he is not a master who robs them of their individual autonomy, or leaves them stranded outside of culturally meaningful social roles. This kind of leadership stood in stark contrast to the Omrid monarchs, whose authority was also rooted in a claim to represent Yahweh, and yet showed no respect for the lives and culture of hill-country villagers.

The Prophets and Their Stories in Hegemonic Struggle

Prophets in ancient Israel offered an alternative source of leadership and power to Israelite villagers, probably in much the same way that they do to Middle Eastern clans and villages today (see Hill, Chapter 2 above). Stories about prophets may have been wielded like political swords in deadly rivalries between villages and clans in ancient Israel, each group claiming the most miracles performed by their prophet. Then, under the extreme social crisis of the Omrid monarchy, stories about the prophets Elijah and Elisha became associated with Jehu, the young army commander who toppled the Omrids in a sweeping revolt and established his own regime.

The relationship of the stories about Elijah and Elisha and the historical "reality" of these prophets is difficult to untangle and impossible to know for sure; however, it is useful to make some educated guesses. First, the stories' content and narrative form give clues as to how they originated and to how and why they were disseminated. They appear to have originated through actual interactions with prophets, and their content indicates that these relationships empowered the people who formed a personal transactional relationship with the prophet and who then told others about that relationshiop through a story. It is possible that these relationships were not actually contracted with a live prophet, but with some shrine or memorial place associated with him. Here people may have felt that they interacted with the prophet just as contemporary Mexican peasants feel that they form relationships with saints through statues of these saints.

This kind of relationship with a prophet was an anti-monarchic practice because (1) it gave people access to the gods via a personal relationship with a figure with whom one could negotiate, as opposed to the impersonal, hierarchical religion offered by a state monarchy, and (2) it was intrinsically Yahwistic, a practice rooted in hill-country life and traditions.

Thus, the stories probably began as first-person narratives, told by people who actually experienced a "miracle" of personal transformation with a prophet. However, once out of the personal sphere, such stories may have been used by families, clans, and other factions to foster their own political and social status. The Shunammite story provides a case for tentatively sketching out how this process may have worked. This woman may have formed a relationship with the prophet whom she believed benefited her personally by giving her a son and keeping that son from dying. She then may have passed this story on to members of her family and introduced them to the prophet. The various family members, in turn, may have told these stories to members of other clans, building up the reputations of both family and prophetic patron. This kind of propoganda could have been used then to claim rights to particular tracts of land or political offices.

Beyond the level of the stories, exactly what the roles of the historical Elijah and Elisha were in the anti-Omrid social foment that led to the Jehu revolt is impossible to reconstruct. However, it appears that the prophet Elijah gained credibility as the authentic voice of Yahwism within a large sector of the population during Ahab's reign, probably attracting masses of Israelites who were eager to rally around a prophet who, the stories assured them, could feed them and make them feel in control of their lives again. It is probable that Elijah, as a Yahwist cult leader, drew his ideas from traditional folk religion, employing symbols and language comfortable to peasants, common people, and other traditional Yahwists, including some regional elites.

Whether or not Elisha actually was a legitimate successor to Elijah is impossible to know. It is clear, however, that Elisha inherited Elijah's literary legacy, both oral and written. Todd (Chapter 1 above) demonstrates this with her outline of the process of the incorporation of the Elijah stories into a literary cycle arranged by the Jehu regime to demonstrate continuity between Elijah and Elisha. In this way, Elisha's supporters managed to have their prophet designated as the voice of authentic Yahwism for the new regime, and Jehu's supporters linked themselves to two groups of traditional Yahwists—the anti-Omrid rural elites and the disenfranchised villagers.

Another way to conceptualize Elisha's role in the Jehu regime is as a royal prophet, or a middleman. Wilson argues along these lines that Elisha became a part of the royal establishment (69–206). However, he describes this as a shift in role from that of peripheral prophet who communicated the aspirations of powerless individuals to the "larger society" to that of a central prophet who performed "social maintenance functions for the crown" (Wilson: 69–71).

Furthermore, Wilson insightfully suggests that after Elijah there was a deliberate counter-attempt to portray the peripheral prophet in a more central role, allied with royal authority as part of an effort to suppress anti-royal prophetic activity. While Wilson implies that this was a necessary move to maintain social order for the good of the whole Israelite society, he indirectly provides an explanation for a more conflict-oriented interpretation of this counter-attempt. He states that "as part of this process the prophetic word was elevated to the status of Torah with the result that the prophet was assigned as much authority as Moses" (Wilson: 201). Reinterpreted within the context of this essay, Wilson's insight suggests that the ruling class of Jehu's regime established a new religious intermediary role between royal family and village. While prophets had traditionally represented village and tribal interests to the king, they now would occupy a more ambiguous role as middlemen (cf. F.G. Bailey: 167, 176), balancing their own political interests between those of the ruling elite and those of the villages. Their writings would become part of the authoritative national canon of religious literature, despite their often critical attitude toward the monarchy and the urban upper classes.

The differing roles of Elijah and Elisha that later literary arrangements of the stories have tried to erase may represent the difference between the earlier, traditional role of prophet as speaker for the grievances of rural villagers, both wealthy and poor, and the new middleman role of prophet as "go-between," directing and controlling the processes by which the village political structures become integrated into the state political structure. It appears that both prophets came from peasant backgrounds.[13] However, it is possible that Elijah was the only true spokesperson for a message of resistance against the state and its exploitation, one rooted in both peasant and regional elite discontent with the Omrids. By contrast, Elisha may have merely adopted Elijah as his predecessor in order to legitimate his own role as a prophet closely allied with the interests of the state. In this case, however, it was a state with a new ruler, Jehu, who promised to represent the interests of traditional Yahwists, both peasant and elite.

The new Jehuid state needed middlemen like Elisha, men who were adept at juggling hegemonic language, and who could convince different factions and classes that their own ways of life and belief were being represented by the ruling elite and the new state form of Yahwism. Their task was a complex one, mediating tensions between multiple groups that included (1) the king and his party, which supported an agrarian system and a mode of production allowing them to live off peasant labor, and which supported the present kings' claims to be a true Yahwist; (2) the rural elites who had opposed Omri and supported Jehu, and who similarly did not want major changes in the agrarian system except perhaps a decrease in the centralized power of the royal family; and (3) vil-

---

[13] Elijah is introduced in 1 Kgs 17:1 in a textually ambiguous way, which may indicate that he came from peasant settlers in Gilead (Chaney, oral communication). Elisha was recruited by Elijah while plowing (1 Kgs 19:19), which may be a later gloss but may also indicate he is a peasant (even though his plowing with 12 oxen is clearly an addition to the story).

lage peasants still trying to maintain traditional lifestyles with peasant modes of production and peasant religious orientations.

Prophets continued in this role of middlemen and mediators of various Yahwistic hegemonies and counter-hegemonies until the Assyrian invasion of Israel. Whatever their allegiances, the prophets were all steeped in the various discourses of Yahwism, and were adept at manipulating this language for the purposes they felt compelled to defend. It is probable that different prophets represented the interests and perspectives of different factions and groups, some more resistant to state power than others. In the case discussed here, Elijah appears in the more traditional role associated with the prophetic tradition—that of the voice of resistance to injustice and the abuse of power in the name of Yahwism. Elisha, on the other hand, appears to have sided more with the state, perhaps because he genuinely believed the Jehu regime would fulfill its claims more justly in light of Yahwism.

The Stories as Monarchic Legitimation

As Todd demonstrates (Chapter 1 above), the Jehu regime found it politically imperative to preserve stories about Elijah as part of their legitimation after the overthrow of the Omrids. The Elisha material was probably preserved in a similar fashion after the revolt for the same reasons. This incorporation of the prophetic cycles into the monarchic state literature indicates that the Jehu faction wanted to legitimate Elisha as the bearer of the Yahwistic legacy of Elijah. This appears to be an example of what Hill identifies as the cooptation of a "local hero" by a central structure (Chapter 2 above). It was accomplished by taking living, changing, oral stories adapted and circulated by people in their daily political and personal struggles, and petrifying them into a written structure that legitimized only one political struggle, that of the Jehu elites.

Accordingly, it is possible—my earlier discussion of the prophetic role notwithstanding—that an actual historical figure named Elisha had little or nothing to do with the Jehu revolution. The Jehu faction/clan may have struggled and schemed to overthrow the Omrids using pragmatic methods of political maneuvering and warfare, and then justified itself according to the Yahwistic traditions with stories about how Jehu had been divinely anointed by Elisha (2 Kgs 9: 1–13), and how Elisha was the successor of the popular anti-Baal prophet Elijah (2 Kgs 2:9–18).[14]

The variety of stories that were preserved as part of this legitimation includes both stories that involve the elite and stories that involve peasants, women, and other marginalized people. The elite stories plainly lent themselves to Jehu's ideological strategies. Many of them show Elijah and Elisha in historical roles against Omrid kings and Baal worshipers, and helping armies and upper class people. These include (1) punishment of Omrid kings (2 Kgs 3: 4–17,20; 1 Kgs 21); (2) restoration of land from crown seizure (2 Kgs 8:1–6); (3) military victories against Aram (2 Kgs 13:14–19, 24-25; 2 Kgs 7:3–20); and (4) replacing Baalism with Yahwism (1 Kgs 18:17–46). The prophets stand out in these stories as well-matched adversaries of kings, not as accessible enablers of powerless widows and peasants. Elisha is closely associated here with the elite military image of chariots and horses (2 Kgs 2; 6:15–24), not the slings and arrows of a simple village chief.

All these were themes and roles appropriate to the new regime's purposes. These elite stories could be selected easily from the many stories that undoubtedly circulated. However, the selection of the simpler miracle stories that represent the concerns and activities of certain disenfranchised groups is more difficult to explain and certainly ironic in terms of the conflict of the hegemonies in Israel. These simple stories reflect a cultural reality, a way of seeing the world, that has nothing to do with a monarchic reality and therefore seems out of place in the monarchic literature. The well-fed and the powerful would not be interested in stories about prophets who help people feed themselves and give them power in their lives, unless there was a politically cogent reason to associate themselves as supporters of such an enabling prophet.

First, it is possible that these stories were chosen because of cultural values which are not directly alluded to in the available sources. For example, it is possible that Yahwistic tradition at the time included a strong community norm about obligations towards widows and children, which was reflected more directly in the later prophetic literature.

---

[14] Comaroff (1978) describes a similar practice. He explains how "ascriptive rules" are used in political scrambles over the chiefship both as resources to assert one's own legitimacy and validate one's own actions, but also as a code to comprehend the complexities of everyday political action. "Winning the chiefship is a matter of achievement . . . gained largely by controlling resources and capabilities which are extrinsic to formal institutional arrangements. Yet such outcomes are rationalized in entirely ascriptive terms; the successful competitor *becomes* the rightful heir" (16).

Thus stories about widows and childless women may have stirred up great feelings of indignation and injustice, precisely because women and children were considered the most vulnerable in traditional Israelite society.

Another possibility is that these tales may have been incorporated as part of a propaganda campaign for motherhood and increased population, which might have suited the purposes of a new regime that intended to continue policies that would expand both production and reproduction as part of their attempts to expand their wealth. It is not clear, however, whether or not increased population was desirable at this point in Israel's history.

A more compelling argument for their inclusion, providing an interesting insight into the complexity of hegemonic struggles, is the following. Women who interact with the prophet are shown at the conclusion of the stories confirmed in their roles both as prophetic patronesses and as mothers. Stories like this may have been chosen because women could have formed a significant political force as patronesses of the Yahwist prophets and needed to be acknowledged in the Jehu literature.

An analysis that incorporates an understanding of the cultural construction of gender suggests an additional reason for the inclusion of so many stories about women who are empowered by the Yahwistic prophet to return to their roles as successful mothers. As Todd (see Chapter 1 above) illustrates, the Jehu writers of the Elijah cycle portray Jezebel, the Phoenician wife of Ahab, as the primary perpetrator of corrupt Baalism. They paint a portrait of a manipulative foreign woman, a Baal-worshipping virago who corrupts the Israelite king who marries her. Thus by making Jezebel the major culprit for Omrid corruption—the woman behind the throne—they distance the role of monarch from the idea that monarchy, by its very nature, is a threat to traditional Israel. Rather, what these cycles suggest is that what corrupts Israel are not monarchs but marriages to women like Jezebel—foreign women—who reach for power outside this designated patriarchal pattern.

Furthermore, when juxtaposed with the miracle stories' portraits of virtuous Yahwist wives and mothers reaching only for power within the context of their families' needs, the prophetic cycles serve an additional hegemonic role for the Jehu regime. First, it is possible that women gained some political leverage and power in relationship to Elijah and/or Elisha, who needed them for financial, material support, or who may have genuinely made room for more flexible roles for women in their followings. However, the Jehu military faction that came into power, headed up by male warriors, was unlikely to have been sympathetic to women in non-traditional roles and probably eager to restore members of that sex to their proper Yahwistic roles.

Of course these men may not have been conscious of these hegemonic motives for keeping women in their place. They may have genuinely believed that women with political power corrupt men, as witnessed by what happened to Ahab when he let a woman manipulate the throne. But this is precisely what Williams (88) means by "hegemony" as a sense of "absolute because experienced reality." As men who had grown up in a patriarchal culture, they assumed that male dominance was normal and female dominance, as exemplified by Jezebel, was abnormal and ultimately ruinous to Israel.

Therefore, it is clear that although this was a revolt benefiting some groups, the patriarchal structure of Yahwism was not overturned in favor of an egalitarian social order with women offered equal access to public power. I do not mean to imply that women in the urban monarchic culture of the Omrids were actually treated more equally than in Yahwist, rural culture. The point is that within the literarily-mediated struggles between these dominant and counter-hegemonies, evidence is embedded of another struggle between women's realities and two different male power structures.

The reasons for preserving stories about Elisha's core group of followers seem more obvious than those proposed for the women's stories. If Elisha was raised to a priestly role in the state through his support of the Jehu revolution, then he undoubtedly brought his core followers with him into positions of influence. These stories describe the mutually beneficial role between Elisha and his core group and demonstrate their leadership abilities, particularly in the area of feeding masses of people. Such stories of restored inedible stews and miraculously expanding food supplies would be an appropriate theme for a new regime trying to legitimate its power to a people who were suffering and starving from the policies of the former regime.

It is interesting that there are no stories preserved in these texts about other marginalized peoples, such as prostitutes, beggars, or simple day laborers who were not affiliated with the core followers of Elisha, even though such groups undoubtedly formed part of the agrarian social structure. It is probable that stories about their interactions with a prophet would not have been included because it was difficult to reconcile them with the new elite's political and religious strategies. Stories about these members from the bottom rung of this agrarian society would serve no purpose to a ruling family who did not plan to restructure the state, much less return it to a more decentralized and egalitarian tribal village system without such an expendable class.

It appears, then, that stories were selected for inclusion in the Jehu level cycles because of their compatability with the ideological strategies of the new regime. The Jehu elites were trying to establish themselves as the legitimate inheritors and defenders of Yahwism, which they intended to perpetuate not simply as what we would think of as an "ideology," but as an entire structure of subordination and domination. This included the mode of production as much as it included the ideas that saturated and supported that mode of production. This hegemony, in order to be all-encompassing and dominant, had to incorporate both elite experiences and concerns as well as those of the peasants and women who had fueled Elijah's Yahwistic movement. It had to appear to be a hegemony of true Yahwism, the legitimate inheritor of Israelite village traditions that were important to both non-Omrid elites as well as disenfranchised peasants and women, each in their own distinctive way.

However, despite the Jehu party's strategy to legitimize themselves as true Yahwists, later prophets like Amos and Hosea condemned the Jehu dynasty for corruption and deviation from Yahwist traditions equal to that of the Omrids. Under such continuing oppressive conditions, the anti-monarchic genre of prophetic miracle stories undoubtedly continued to thrive as a source of personal and political enpowerment in the face of monarchic hegemony.

Conclusion

These stories about Elijah and Elisha, recorded in the Jehu legitimation cycle and then in the Deuteronomist's late kingdom literature, are elements of a folklore that has been recorded, redacted, shaped and reshaped as part of a complex tradition discourse that emerged over a thousand-year period. The prophet is depicted within this tradition through the bits of northern tradition in the Deuteronomist's texts and throughout the later prophetic works as the Yahwistic representative of different counter-hegemonies, to various degrees critical of the monarchic state.

However, the dissenting voice of the prophet needs to be understood as arising within a specific historical context. It appears that prophets emerged in Israel as it evolved from a relatively egalitarian clan confederation into a complex, hierarchical state. Some of the earliest roles in which they are depicted—within the Elijah and Elisha miracle stories—show them as local Yahwistic leaders who gained support from various disenfranchised groups of Israelites, particularly women from both the rural elite and the peasantry, as well as peasant men. It appears that this role shifted with Elisha's involvement in the Jehu regime. As the more sophisticated stories of the Elijah-Elisha cycles illustrate, the prophet seems to have become increasingly involved as a mediator between elite factions, not simply the voice of peasant Yahwism.

Thus, the prophets provided a cultural resource to differing groups of people at various historical periods for making political claims and for demonstrating resistance to whatever dominant hegemony threatened the integrity of a particular way of life. The language of resistance that they wielded with authority—Yahwism—likewise evolved and changed in the context of hegemonic struggles, as reflected in redactive studies of the biblical texts. In order to understand how particular prophets and their messages make sense in the scheme of Israelite history, it is useful to see them in socio-cultural context, as shaped by the constraints of the wider political-economic structure and shifts in the mode of production caused by state and interstate social dynamics.

Thus, these Elijah-Elisha miracle stories provide fruitful ground for the concerns of both contemporary anthropologists and biblical scholars. In terms of current cultural anthropology's interests, the stories provide a case study where historical material and textual/cultural analysis can be combined to yield insights into the multiple dynamics involved in counter-hegemonic struggles. In terms of biblical studies, the stories furnish an opportunity to demonstrate what new synthetic approaches in cultural anthropology can contribute to understanding the meaning of a text formerly considered obscure.

4

The Prophetic Alternative: Elisha and the Israelite Monarchy

WESLEY J. BERGEN

Introduction

The stories concerning Elisha the prophet, as they presently stand in the Deuteronomistic History (hereafter DtrH), can function to bolster two ideological motifs, the conflict of which does not allow either to be presented fully. The first motif is the narration of the events following the triumph of Elijah, a victory of the forces of Yahweh over the evil king Ahab, and especially over the Phoenician influence of Jezebel and her prophets of Baal. This triumph is shown through the period of relative theological peace that follows in the Elisha narrative.[1] Second, this unit continues the narrative fiction claiming that kingship is the only form of political power acceptable to Yahweh. It is possible historically that the prophets represented an alternative form of social organization to that of kingship. Nevertheless, in almost all instances, DtrH portrays the prophets in a way that does not usurp the political authority of the king.

---

[1] By "Elisha narrative" I refer to any stories which make reference to Elisha. I am not maintaining that this is a separate literary unit, but rather a section of the DtrH which can be set apart by its reference to a specific individual.

Our text thus shows both the "naturalness" of the voice that subjugates the prophet and the cracks that can be heard in this voice.

My thesis is that the dominant voice[2] of our text tries, with relative success, to undermine Elisha as a potential leader of an authentic alternative to the political and social structures of monarchy. This is despite the text's incessantly negative attitude toward all northern kings and the generally positive portrayals of individual prophets as authentic messengers of Yahweh.

As in any monarchial state, the king represents the highest form of power. At least this is true for those who recognize the legitimacy of monarchic power, and especially for those who are involved in the processes and actions of this social system. The realm of monarchic power claims to extend over and above all other realms of power. The exception in DtrH is the realm of the Mosaic Law, the realm of Yahweh. As a representative of Yahweh, the prophet occupies a place of high authority, a definite threat to the claims of monarchy.

Within this context, the text undertakes the Herculean task of portraying the prophet as the legitimate spokesperson of Yahweh while not allowing the prophet to intrude upon monarchic power. One is tempted to suggest that it cannot possibly succeed. However, in view of the fact that most modern commentators have uncritically accepted this view of history, it has succeeded admirably.

The relationship between monarchic and prophetic power needs careful examination. Our text is not univocal in its presentation of prophetic power. These two forms of power coexist within one text, but do not do so comfortably. At points the text relegates prophetic power to a marginal role within a society dominated by monarchic power. At other points prophetic power eclipses monarchy.

This essay will look at various sections of the Elisha narrative and examine with ideologically suspicious eyes the success or failure of the text in regard to its desired portrayal of the social realities of ancient Israel. I will examine the cracks and crevices that appear in the narrative and their relationship to the dominant voice in the text. As well, I will

---

[2] I am using "dominant voice" here to express the plurivocal nature of any text. Whether these "voices" reside in the text, the reader, or a reading community, within a particular reading community a certain consensus can often be surmised concerning "what the text really means." The existence of such a consensus suggests that the text has certain dominant ideas or motifs, or at least has been read as such in a particular historical context. This paper is an attempt to "listen" to the other "voices" in the Elisha narrative.

look for evidence of alternate visions of Israelite society that the dominant voice is unable to subjugate fully.³

Method

The Elisha narrative is one attempt to work through a major political conflict in ancient Israelite society. To say that this conflict is worked through in our text is not to divorce it from a historical milieu. The conflicts within the text are a figuration of the conflicts within Israelite society (cf. Bal: 3). This is certainly a historical struggle, the struggle over political systems, over economic systems, over the relationship of a people to Yahweh. The history of Israel is inscribed within its texts whether or not these texts naively reflect "real events."

The realization that there are cracks or inconsistencies within the biblical text has a long history. In historical critical exegesis, it is one of the bases of source criticism. What separates my investigation from source-critical ones is that I will not divide the text into various units, which might represent different traditions. Rather, the inconsistencies will be read as signs of the inconsistencies within the ideology that dominates the text.

The Elisha narratives serve as a focal point for the ideological tremors which resonate through DtrH. Any reader of the Elisha narrative will find that coherence is elusive in 2 Kings. If coherence remains outside the grasp of the reader, we may assume that it remained outside the grasp of the writer(s) as well—and this despite their efforts to achieve it. This being the case, it makes the most sense to argue that the a-coherence (not incoherence, which suggests weak writing skills) reflects the inadequacy of their ideology. That is, we are dealing not with one ideology versus another, but rather with a single ideology failing to provide the completeness it claims for itself. Up to this point in DtrH, history has been moving along relatively smoothly. The coming of Elisha proves the veneer of coherence cannot hide the basic flaws underneath.

---

³ The concept of subjugated knowledge is developed by Foucault, *Power\Knowledge*, pp.81ff.

Direct Confrontations

1. Dialogue in the Desert: 2 Kings 3:13–20

This chapter describes the attempt of the king of Israel to reestablish control of Moab through military conquest, with the aid of Judah and Edom. This particular king of Israel, Jehoram, is judged overall negatively by the narrator (3:2,3), despite positive comparison to his father.

The scene is set as a rather normal battle for a king of Israel. The account begins as a purely secular recollection (vv. 4–9). There is no hint of a concern for Yahweh's involvement until the armies run out of water (v. 10). Surprisingly, it is the king of Israel[4] who speaks the message of Yahweh for himself and the other kings. It is Jehoshaphat, king of Judah, who suggests the possibility of inquiring of a prophet. Elisha's response to their questioning is directed at the king of Israel and is a rejection of the questioner. The king of Israel repeats his declaration of Yahweh's will, which can be read as a challenge to Elisha's exclusive right to do so. Nevertheless, Elisha inquires of Yahweh, and receives assurance of miraculous deliverance and ultimate victory.

Elisha's presence in this scene is itself interesting. There are no precedents (except for the polyfunctional Moses) for prophetic accompaniment of battle expeditions. The profane tone of the early part of the scene would fit well into modern historiography, and the change of orientation preplexes the reader who ponders the role of Elisha.

Elisha helps the kings out of their difficulty by virtue of his *alternate* form of power. He instructs the kings in the methods of conquest. However, he uses his power in the service of, and thus as subordinate to, monarchic power. He is there when the kings need him. He is presented as subjugating prophetic power under the realm of monarchic power. Elisha plays his appointed role, well within the limits monarchic power would ascribe to a prophet.

Verses 26 and 27 add a disquieting note to this story. The smooth movement from prophecy to fulfilment, or from attack to victory, is interrupted by a break in the chronological sequence. The battle that was over (v. 25) is now still in progress (v. 26); the victory that was won is now lost. We are left with the uncomfortable sense that something has gone wrong. The text affords no resolution to our discomfort. However, Elisha's prediction of victory (v. 19) is fulfilled (v. 25), the reversal focus-

---

4 After v.6 Jehoram is merely referred to by his title. Jehoshaphat of Judah continues to be named. The use or absence of names functions to depersonalize the kings, creating a stereotypical "king of Israel."

ing on the actions of the kings. Thus, the discordant ending serves to reduce our estimation of monarchic power.

2. *Healing of Naaman (5:1–27)*

A study of the role of the king of Israel in this story defines clearly the ambiguity of his presence for Dtr. If we would arbitrarily remove vv.4–8 from the text, thereby extracting the king, the story would still be coherent. These verses add little to the plot, and play no role in the fabula. What they do is provide for the king to be part of this international meeting, however ineffective his presence appears. The king's panic (v. 7) continues to remind us that he is not a good king, but his presence also perpetuates the fiction that kings are necessary. Thus, instead of Elisha coming to the aid of a foreign commander, we have Elisha coming to the aid of the king of Israel—although he does so from a position of strength, having a form of power superior to the king's.

To characterize the power relationship between king and prophet to this point, one might say that prophetic power is different from monarchic power in kind, but that monarchic power is characterized as having complete control within its own sphere of influence. When the story relates incidents in the jurisdiction of the king, the prophet comes to the king's aid, and does not function to usurp his power. In this way the prophet is like any other artisan. The smith is also superior to the king in his ability to make swords, but the smith makes swords for the king's use.

Neverless, the possibility of a society based on prophetic leadership emerges in places such as this, despite the attempts of the dominant voice to subjugate it. The story of the ancient struggle between different forms of power emerges, as prophetic power controls an international confrontation. The fact that we could read the king right out of this and other texts suggests that monarchic power is really unnecessary. Royal power is repeatedly characterized as weak and ineffective, while the prophet can bring victory, healing, and even life.

3. *Arameans Attacking Samaria (6:24–7:20)*

This text demonstrates many of the same principles as the one above. The story is of the Aramean invasion of Israel, the siege of Samaria, and the consequent starvation. Elisha predicts the end of the siege and the retreat of the Arameans, saving the city from defeat. Again, prophetic power is shown to be superior in kind to monarchic power, as the anxious king comes running to Elisha. Elisha again acts to aid the king, although this direct intention is not ascribed to him. Elisha's superior power does not threaten the king's position, nor does his connection with the elders. However, the possibility of political confrontation emerges in the king's ineffectiveness in dealing with the situation, and in the portrayal of Elisha's house as the true location of power.

Some aspects of this story also add to our picture. The narrative follows the assertion in 6:23 that the Arameans no longer raided Israel after the miracle of Elisha at Dothan. The presence of a battle report at this point undermines prophetic power, and suggests that it is really unable to ensure national security. If prophetic power is attempting to claim status as a true alternative to monarchic power, the ordering of the stories seriously undermines this claim.

It is also important to note that Elisha only acts after being threatened. This places in doubt the nature of his power. Is he able to cause the flight of the Arameans, or at least to influence the actions of Yahweh to bring this about? Or can he only predict—in which case his power is quite limited? If he was able to cause this flight, why did he not act before things deteriorated to this point?

These questions illustrate further the larger relationship between prophetic and monarchic power in the story. Prophetic power undermines and even embarrasses monarchic power, but it is ultimately useful to it. While the conflict of political and social systems that underlies the stories continues to intrude, the dominant voice of the text wishes to remove this conflict far from our minds.

4. Minor Indications

4:13 suggests that the prophet can influence the king in regard to the Shunammite woman, as he proves able to do in 8:1–6. This does not imply superiority, for they could simply be close friends. This type of connection places Elisha firmly within the usual domain of monarchic power. The story conscripts Elisha into the power structures that surround the monarchy, thus domesticating him, robbing him of his ability to represent an alternative power *structure*. From within the structures of monarchic power, he can only represent an alternative avenue, not an alternative system, of power.

4:42 presents a different perspective. The offering of the first fruits that is brought to Elisha presents him as an alternative to the royal cultus in Samaria. This directly challenges monarchic power, for religious and political authority are closely connected in DtrH. However, since this particular incident supplants the religious authority of Samaria, which the narrator consistently judges as evil since it subverts the primacy of Jerusalem, this threat to monarchic power is not a threat to DtrH's larger purpose. Nonetheless, this is an important passage in our study. It illustrates the challenge that prophetic power may have posed to monarchic power. Stories such as this represent a break in the attempt by the dominant textual voice to present itself as "natural," as the only possible option.

6:20–23 echoes the theme of prophetic power as superior in kind but still subordinate to monarchic power. The Arameans have attempted to capture Elisha. He has struck the army with blindness, and has led them into Samaria, where the king of Israel anxiously requests Elisha's counsel. The king's question to Elisha in v. 21 illustrates our point well: "My father, shall I slay them, shall I slay them?" If the question was "What are *you* going to do with them?", the king would be shown in a subordinate position. Here, however, the king is the one who needs to make the decision. Again, he is weak and indecisive, but it is still his decision.

13:14–19 provides us with the final illustration of the theme of the subordination of prophetic power. The king's attitude towards Elisha's impending death, as well as the aid Elisha gives in the upcoming battles against Hazael, demonstrate the important function Elisha has played in the eyes of the text. The story conceives this importance in terms of the king. Elisha will be missed because of his valuable service to royal power.

Succession Passages

The succession passages function as the primary historical signposts along the way, giving us a time-frame in which to view the story. They are particularly instructive in a text that often omits the name of the particular king who is part of the story. In many ways, they appear as intrusions into the stories of Elisha's activities. As intrusions, they return to the political historiography of the listing of undistinguished kings, which both precedes and follows the stories of Elijah and Elisha.

At first the succession passages appear to function as reminders that monarchic power is what is truly important in this society. However, if this is their function, they are notable failures, for the historiography contained therein is an amazing mishmash of names and relative dates. Below is an outline of the history presented in these passages. To help keep the various people straight, I will put the kings of Judah in *italics* and underline the kings of Israel.

The story begins with Ahaziah, son of Ahab, king of Israel, falling through the floor of his house and dying. He is replaced (1:17,18) by Jehoram, his brother, during the reign of *Jehoram*, king of Judah. Jehoram then re-takes the throne (not having lost it) a few years earlier, during the reign of *Jehoshaphat*, king of Judah (3:1-3), father of *Jehoram*, king of Judah (whose reign is presumably later). *Jehoshaphat* then disappears from the text, and *Jehoram*, his son, takes the throne of Judah, during the reign of Joram (sic) of Israel, son of Ahab. *Jehoram* is also the son-in-law of Ahab (8:16-19).

Joram (sic) of Judah then dies in one of the most bizarre battle accounts ever recorded, so *Ahaziah*, son of *Jehoram* (sic), becomes king, during the reign of Joram, king of Israel (8:25-27). At this point, the least one would expect is a commercial break, but instead both Joram and *Ahaziah* are killed (9:23-28), and Jehu, son of Jehoshaphat (not the same one as above), becomes king in Israel (9:13), and *Ahaziah* (again?) becomes king in Judah (9:29).

At this point, it should be obvious that the narrator has no intention of conveying to us any kind of realistic history. In fact, quite the opposite would seem to be true. The narrator seems to go out of his way to convince us that history as political/military chronology is not the point. The intrusion of the prophets into DtrH has caused a rupture in "normal" history.

Presumably it might be possible to reconstruct and harmonize these bits of history into some kind of recognizable shape.[5] But we might also assume that the authors/redactors of this text had the intelligence to do this themselves if they had thought it important.

The text seems to spare no detail in confusing or combining the kings of Judah and Israel. Yet on the surface, the formulas we expect for an orderly account of the handing down of kingship are basically intact. This superficial order, combined with deep-seated confusion, suggests that the disorder is significant to our understanding of the relationships of power in the text.

Let me take this idea one step further. It might be reasonable to suggest that the narrator in fact wishes to convince us that this entire story does not take place within history as we usually perceive it. Rather, these

---

[5] A recent example of reconstruction is Hayes and Hooker: 26-32. They devote an entire chapter to Jehoram and Ahaziah, hypothesizing only one Jehoram, king of both Judah and Israel.

events take place in some sort of never-never land, where kings are unimportant, and things happen for entirely different reasons.

Elisha's presence in the text not only breaks up the flow of "natural" political historiography but breaks up history itself. Earlier Elijah has been called the "disturber of Israel" (1 Kgs 18:17). Elisha takes this disturbance one step further, distorting usual time sequence with his presence.

Whether or not this confusion is intentional, the text leaves us with a powerful though subtle message about the importance of kings, and the way Yahweh acts in history. Yahweh's actions, or those of the prophet, act as disruption, changing not only situations but reality. Yahweh is not just a force who has power over nature. Yahweh's power is beyond nature, beyond time.

In this way, the text gives us a counter-indication to its usual proclamation of the "naturalness" of kingship and the subsidiary nature of prophetic power. The prophetic intrusion into history is the intrusion of Yahweh, and the history of kingship must take a back seat to this event. It is kingship that is portrayed as secondary, and unworthy of clear recording.

Elisha's Message

As we have seen above, the prophet Elisha is not presented as a threat to the monarchic power structure. Nonetheless, as the successor to Elijah, and as someone bearing the title of "prophet," we would expect Elisha to challenge verbally the actions of the kings and/or the people. Elijah is well known for his famous challenge, "If Yahweh is God, follow him; but if Baal, follow him" (1 Kgs 18:21). It is for this reason that it is so very surprising to discover that Elisha has no message. Elisha never addresses the people, neither does he send messages to the kings advising them of correct conduct. He does not confront the prophets of other gods, nor the "false" prophets of his own god. He does not link healing with obedience, or death with disobedience. It might even be said that Elisha's god is one without demands or expectations of any kind. Yahweh knows what is going to happen, and can change things at will. But this will is not connected to any ethical or legal code. It simply exists.

So what has changed? Where has the message of Elijah gone? How have we moved from "Is it because there is no God in Israel..." (Elijah, 1:3) to "... that he may know that there is a prophet in Israel" (Elisha, 5:8)?

The change in role for the prophet Elisha is paralleled by his change in status within Israelite society. Elijah is an outsider in most senses of the term. He comes from Tishbe, Gilead, across the Jordan. He spent his life on the geographical edges of Israel, or outside its borders. Further, Elijah is presented as a loner, a person who acts alone and does little to draw support to himself.

On the other hand, Elisha lives either in the cities of Israel, or with the communities of "the sons of the prophets." He is presented as being in the company of the elders of Samaria (6:32) or living in Dothan (6:13). In this way he appears as part of Israelite society.

This difference can be set parallel to the differences in message. Elijah is in direct conflict with the monarchic system, with its pretensions of power. As an outsider, however, he is unable to represent a stable alternative social structure. He is merely one individual railing against the evils within the monarchy.

Elisha, as part of Israelite society, can represent an alternative stable society. He can be studied as an option of how a non-monarchic system might function. Thus, any challenge that Elisha directs at the king could also be read as a challenge to the monarchic system itself. A text that presents Elisha in direct confrontation with royal power can be seen as a conflict between two systems, exactly the scenario the text wishes to avoid at all costs. The conflict between the monarchic and prophetic *systems* is outside the fiction the text has set up, and which it must maintain at all costs.

For this reason Elisha is a prophet with no message. We see a prophet who goes about, or rather sits at home, performing miracles in the name of the silent Yahweh. He lives in a time when the kings are judged negatively by the narrator, yet ethical change is of no concern to him. He is allowed no ethical challenge in order to blunt his political challenge.

There is a further reason for the lack of message from Elisha. Elisha must be shown as a failure. Elisha must fail in order to compensate for the success of Elijah in bringing Israel back to Yahweh. If Elisha continues the success of Elijah, we might end up with a story in which Israel is judged more positively than Judah. This cannot happen within the historical fiction of DtrH.

Thus, in its presentation of the history of the prophet Elisha, our text risks numerous internal contradictions as it attempts to portray a prophet of Yahweh as a successful presence of Yahweh's power without usurping the political superiority of the (usually evil) monarchic institution. If Elisha continues to admonish and even threaten the kings, then prophetic power might be read as a real political alternative to monarchic power. Neither option is acceptable. The kings of Israel must be humbled, but the prophets need to be put in their place. This place is one of largely cooperative subordination to monarchic power.

Conclusion

The success or failure of the prophets depends largely on the criteria used to judge their goals and role. In the absence of specific judgements by the narrator, judgment is placed in the hands of the reader. This is especially true given the limited frame of reference we receive for the mission of the prophet Elisha. His role is never clearly spelled out, except in continuing the mission of Elijah. Insofar as Elisha completes the three tasks Yahweh assigned to Elijah (1 Kgs 19:15–17, fulfilled in 2 Kgs 8:7–15; 9:1,2), we can judge him a success. The rest of Elisha's activities remain open to interpretation insofar as Elisha lacks a clear mandate.

I have shown that Elisha's role in Israelite society, as defined by the text, is ambiguous, although care is taken never to portray him as a direct threat to the monarchic system. Whether this portrayal is intentional is beyond the scope of this essay. Certainly we can see in this text the remnants of a cultural/political conflict which arose in the history of Israel. It is *this* conflict that is historical and makes the text a reflection of historical events. Again, whether or not the events of the story occurred as written is not our question. While this study is certainly incomplete, I believe a more detailed study will reveal that this conflict permeates the Elisha narrative.

Works Cited

Aharoni, Yohanan and Avi-Yonah, Michael
    1986   *The MacMillan Bible Atlas*. New York: MacMillan.

Ajami, Fouad
    1986   *The Vanished Imam: Musa Al Sadr and the Shia of Lebanon*. New York: Cornell University.

Albright, W.F.
    1942   "A Votive Stele Erected by Ben-Hadad I of Damascus to the God of Melcarth." *BASOR* 87: 23–29.

Alt, Albrecht
    1966   "The Monarchy in Israel and Judah." Pp. 241–59 in *Essays on Old Testament History and Religion*. Trans. by R. A. Wilson. Oxford: Basil Blackwell.

Althusser, Louis
    1970   *Reading Capital*. New York: Pantheon.

Andersen, Francis I.
    1966   "The Socio-Juridical Background of the Naboth Incident." *JBL* 75: 46–57.

Antoun, Richard T.
    1972   "Pertinent Variables in the Environment of Middle Eastern Village Politics: A Comparative Analysis." Pp. 118–63 in *Rural Politics and Social Change in the Middle East*. Eds. R. Antoun and I. Harik. Bloomington: Indiana University.

Augustinovic, A.
    1972   *"El-Khadr" and the Prophet Elijah.* Jerusalem: Franciscan Printing.

Bader, Gershom
    1940   *The Jewish Spiritual Heroes.* New York: Pardes.

Bailey, F.G.
    1969   *Strategems and Spoils: A Social Anthropology of Politics.* New York: Schocken.

Bal, Mieke
    1988   *Death and Dissymmetry.* Chicago: University of Chicago.

Baldensperger, Philip J.
    1894   "Orders of Holy Men in Palestine." *PEFQ* 25: 22-38.
    1913   *The Immovable East.* London: Pitman and Sons.

Bourdieu, Pierre
    1971   *Outline of a Theory of Practice.* Cambridge: Cambridge University.

Bright, John
    1981   *A History of Israel.* 3rd ed. Philadelphia: Westminster.

Brown, Francis; S.R. Driver and Charles A. Briggs, eds.
    1907   *A Hebrew and English Lexicon of the Old Testament.* Oxford: Clarendon.

Brown, John Porter
    1868   *The Darvishes.* London: Frank Cass.

Brown, Peter
    1981   *The Cult of the Saints: Its Rise and Function in Latin Christianity.* Chicago: University of Chicago.
    1982   *Society and the Holy in Late Antiquity.* Berkeley: University of California.

Brown, Raymond E.
    1971   "Jesus and Elisha." *Perspective* [Pittsburgh] 12: 85-104.

Burney, C. F.
    1943   *Notes on the Hebrew Text of the Book of Kings.* Oxford: Clarendon.

Campbell, Antony F.
    1975   *The Ark Narrative: A Form-Critical and Traditio-Historical Study,* SBLDS #16. Missoula, Montana: Scholars Press.

Canaan, Tewfik
    1922   *Studies in Palestinian Customs and Folklore, II: Haunted Springs and Water Demons in Palestine.* Jerusalem: Palestine Oriental Society.
    1924-27   "Mohammedan Saints and Sanctuaries in Palestine." *JPOS* 4: 1–84; 5: 163–203; 6: 1-69, 117–158; 7: 1–88.
    1934   "Modern Palestinian Beliefs and Practice Relating to God." *JPOS* 14: 59–92.

Carlson, R. A.
    1969   "Elie à l'Horeb." *VT* 19: 416–39.
    1970   "Elisee—Le Successeur d'Elie." *VT* 20: 385–405.

Carroll, R. P.
    1969   "The Elijah-Elisha Sagas: Some Remarks on Prophetic Succession in Ancient Israel." *VT* 19: 400–415.

Chaney, Marvin
    1982   "Systemic Study of the Sociology of the Israelite Monarchy." *Semeia* 37: 53–76.
    1983   "Ancient Palestinian Peasant Movements and the Formation of Premonarchic Israel." Pp. 39–90 in *Palestine in Transition: The Emergence of Ancient Israel*. Eds. D. N. Freedman and D. F. Graf. Social World of Biblical Antiquity Series 2. Sheffield: Almond.

Claessen, Henry J. and Peter Skalnik, eds.
    1976   *The Early State: Theories and Hypotheses.* The Hague: Mouton.

Clifford, James
    1988   *The Predicament of Culture: Twentieth Century Ethnography, Literature, and Art.* Cambridge, Mass.: Harvard University.

Cohen, Abner
    1965   *Arab Border-Villages in Israel: A Study of Continuity and Change in Social Organization.* Manchester: Manchester University.

Cohen, G. A.
    1978   *Karl Marx's Theory of History: A Defense.* Princeton: Princeton University.

Cohen, Martin A.
    1975   "In All Fairness to Ahab: A Socio-Political Consideration of the Ahab-Elijah Controversy." *Eretz–Israel* 12: 87–94.

Cohen, Ronald
    1976   "State Origins." Pp. 31–75 in *The Early State: Theories and Hypotheses*. Eds. H. J. Claessen and P. Skalnik. The Hague: Mouton.

Cohen, Ronald and Elman Service
    1978   *Origins of the State: The Anthropology of Political Evolution.* Philadelphia: ISHI.

Collier, Jane Fishburne
    1974   "Women in Politics." Pp. 89–96 in *Woman, Culture, and Society.* Ed. Michelle Z. Rosaldo and Louise Lamphere. Stanford: Stanford University.

Collier, Jane F. and Rosaldo, Michelle Z.
    1981   "Politics and Gender in Simple Societies." Pp. 275–329 in *Sexual Meanings: The Cultural Construction of Gender and Sexuality.* Ed. Sherry B. Ortner and Harriet Whitehead. Cambridge: Cambridge University.

Comaroff, John
    1978   "Rules and Rulers: Political Processes in a Tswana Chiefdom." *Man* 13: 1–20.

Comaroff, Jean
    1985   *Body of Power, Spirit of Resistance: The Culture and History of a South African Chiefdom.* Chicago: University of Chicago

Conder, Claude R.
    1878   *Tent Work in Palestine.* Vol. 2. New York: D. Appleton.

Coote, Robert B.
    1981   "Yahweh Recalls Elijah." Pp. 115–20 in *Traditions in Transformation.* Ed. Baruch Halpern and Jon Levenson. Winona Lake, Indiana: Eisenbrauns.

Coote, Robert B., and Mary P. Coote
    1990   *Power, Politics, and the Making of the Bible: An Introduction.* Minneapolis: Fortress.

Corrington, Gail Peterson
    1985   "Salvation, Celibacy, and Power: Divine Women in Late Antiquity." Seminar paper, SBL.

Cross, Frank Moore
    1972   "The Stele Dedicated to Melcarth by Ben-Hadad of Damascus." *BASOR* 205: 36–42.
    1973   *Canaanite Myth and Hebrew Epic.* Cambridge: Harvard University.

Donaldson, Christopher
    1980   *Martin of Tours: Parish Priest, Mystic, and Exorcist.* London: Routledge and Kegan Paul.

Eikelman, Dale F.
    1981   *The Middle East: An Anthropological Approach.* Englewood Cliffs: Prentice-Hall.

Foucault, Michel
    1980   *Power/Knowledge.* Ed. by Colin Gordon. New York: Pantheon Books.

Frank, Harry Thomas
    1977   *Atlas of the Bible Lands.* Maplewood, New Jersey: Hammond.

Frick, Frank S.
    1986   "Social Science Methods and Theories of Significance for the Study of the Israelite Monarchy: A Critical Review Essay." *Semeia* 37:9–52.

Fried, Morton
    1967   *The Evolution of Political Society: An Essay in Political Anthropology.* New York: Random House.

Gailey, Christine Ward
    1987   *Kinship to Kingship: Gender Hierarchy and State Formation in the Tongan Islands.* Austin: University of Texas.

Geertz, Clifford
    1973   *The Interpretation of Cultures.* New York: Basic Books.

Geertz, Hildred
    1979   "The Meaning of Family Ties." Pp. 356–63 in *Meaning and Order in Moroccan Society.* Ed. H. Geertz and L. Rosen. New York: Cambridge University.

Gellner, Ernest
    1972   "Doctor and Saint." Pp. 307–26 in *Scholars, Saints and Sufis.* Ed. N. Keddie. Berkeley: University of California.

Gilsenan, Michael
    1973   *Saint and Sufi in Modern Egypt: An Essay in the Sociology of Religion.* Oxford: Clarendon.

Goldberg, Harvey
    1988   "Sainthood and Politics in North Africa: The Social Implications of a Muslim-Jewish Idiom." Lecture at University of California, Berkeley.

Gordon, Lucie Duff
    1865 [1991]   *Letters from Egypt.* London: Virago.

Gottwald, Norman
    1976   "Israel, Social and Economic Development of." In *IDB Supp.Vol.* Nashville: Abingdon.

1976a   "Tradition Units and Clusters in Elijah-Elisha Accounts" (ms.).
1976b   An Attempted Typology of Marvel Stories in the Elijah-Elisha Narratives According to Function Components" (ms.).
1979   *The Tribes of Yahweh: A Sociology of the Religion of Liberated Israel 1250–1050 B.C.E.* Maryknoll: Orbis.

Grant, Elihu
1907   *The Peasantry of Palestine: The Life, Manners and Customs of the Village.* Boston: Pilgrim.

Gray, John
1970   *I and II Kings: A Commentary.* 2nd ed. Philadelphia: Westminster.

Green, William Scott
1979   "Palestinian Holy Men: Charismatic Leadership and Rabbinic Tradition." Pp. 619–47 in *Aufstieg und Niedergang der Römischen Welt*, 19.2. New York: Walter de Gruyter.

Greenstein, Edward L.
1988   "On the Genesis of Biblical Prose Narrative." *Prooftexts* 8: 347–63.
1989   *Essays on Biblical Method and Translation.* Atlanta: Scholars.

von Grunebaum, G.E.
1951   *Muslim Festivals.* New York: H. Schuman.

Guillaume, Alfred
1954   *Islam.* New York: Penguin.

Hanauer, J.E.
1904   *Tales Told in Palestine.* Ed. H. G. Mitchell. Cincinnati: Jennings and Graham.

Hanson, John S., and Richard A. Horsley
1985   *Bandits, Prophets, and Messiahs: Popular Movements at the Time of Jesus.* Minneapolis: Winston-Seabury.

Harris, Marvin
1975   *Culture, People, and Nature: An Introduction to General Anthropology.* New York: Crowell.

Hayes, John H., and Paul K. Hooker
1988   *A New Chronology for the Kings of Israel and Judah.* Atlanta: John Knox.

Hayes, John H., and J. Maxwell Miller
1977   *Israelite and Judean History.* Philadelphia: Westminster.

Horsley, Richard A.
    1985   "Like One of the Prophets of Old: Two Types of Popular Prophets at the Time of Jesus." *CBQ* 47: 453–63.

Hussein, Taha
    1981   *An Egyptian Childhood*. Washington, D.C.: Three Continents.

Kapferer, Bruce
    1976   "Introduction: Transactional Models Reconsidered. "Pp. 1–22 in *Transaction and Meaning*. Ed. Bruce Kapferer. Philadelphia: ISHI.

Kautzsch, E., (ed.)
    1910   *Gesenius' Hebrew Grammar*. 2nd ed. Oxford: Clarendon.

Kenyon, Kathleen
    1971   *Royal Cities of the Old Testament*. New York: Schocken.

Khuri, Fuad
    1972   "Sectarian Loyalty Among Rural Migrants in Two Lebanese Suburbs: A Stage Between Family and Nation Allegiance." Pp. 198–213 in *Rural Politics and Social Change in the Middle East*. Ed. R. Antoun and I. Harik. Bloomington: Indiana University.

Kolenkow, Anitra
    1986   "'Divine Men' and Society." *Forum* 2: 85–91.

Lang, Bernhard
    1983   *Monotheism and the Prophetic Minority*. Social World of Biblical Antiquity Series 1. Sheffield: Almond.

Lenski, Gerhard
    1984   *Power and Privilege: A Theory of Social Stratification*. Chapel Hill: University of North Carolina .

Lenski, Gerhard, and Jean Lenski
    1987   *Human Societies: An Introduction to Macrosociology*. 5th ed. New York: McGraw-Hill.

Long, Burke O.
    1973   "The Effect of Divination Upon Israelite Literature." *JBL* 92: 489–97.

Luke, Harry
    1927   *Prophets, Priests, and Patriarchs: Sketches of the Sects of Palestine and Syria*. London: Faith.

Maddin, R., J. D. Muhly, and T. S. Wheeler
    1977   "How the Iron Age Began." *Scientific American* 237: 122–31.

Malamat, A.
　　1973　　"The Aramaeans." Pp. 134–55 in *Peoples of Old Testament Times*. Ed. D. J. Wiseman. Oxford: Clarendon.

Marsot, Afaf Lutfi al-Sayyid
　　1972　　"The Ulama of Cairo in the Eighteenth and Nineteenth Centuries." Pp. 149–66 in *Scholars, Saints, and Sufis*. Ed. N. Keddie. Berkeley: University of California.

Masterman, E. W. G. and R. A. Macalister
　　1915ff　"Tales of Welys and Dervishes." *PEFQ* 46: 171–79; 47: 11–19, 64–71, 126–37, 173–78; 48: 72–80, 119–25, 177–79.

Mazar, Benjamin
　　1962　　"The Aramean Empire and its Relations with Israel." BA 25:97–120. Reprint: pp. 127–51 in *The BAR Reader*. Vol. 2. Missoula, Montana: Scholars. 1965.

Migdal, Joel S.
　　1974　　*Peasants, Politics, and Revolution: Pressures Toward Political and Social Change in the Third World*. Princeton: Princeton University.

Miller, Elaine
　　1973　　*Mexican Folk Narrative from the Los Angeles Area*. American Folklore Society. Austin: University of Texas.

Miller, J. Maxwell
　　1966　　"The Elisha Cycle and the Accounts of the Omride Wars." *JBL* 85: 441–54.
　　1967　　"The Fall of the House of Ahab." *VT* 17: 307–24.
　　1976　　*The Old Testament and the Historian*. Philadelphia: Fortress.

Montgomery, James A.
　　1951　　*A Critical and Exegetical Commentary on the Books of Kings*. New York: Charles Scribner's Sons.

Moore, Barrington, Jr.
　　1966　　*The Social Origins of Dictatorship and Democracy: Lord and Peasant in the Making of the Modern World*. Boston: Beacon.

Napier, B. D.
　　1959　　"The Omrides of Jezreel." *VT* 9: 366–78.

Niditch, Susan
　　1979　　"The Wronged Woman Righted." *HTR* 72: 143–49.

Noel, Daniel C.
　　1990　　"Joseph Campbell: Tuning into Archetypal Telling." Pp. 51–66 in *San Francisco Jung Institute Library Journal*, 9.2: 63.

Oakman, Douglas E.
    1986   *Jesus and the Economic Questions of his Day*. Studies in the Bible and Early Christianity 8. Lewiston: Edwin Mellen.

Ortner, Sherry B.
    1984   "Theory in Anthropology Since the Sixties." *Journal of the Society for Comparative Study of Society and History* 26: 126–66.

Ortner, Sherry B., and Harriet Whitehead
    1981   *Sexual Meanings: The Cultural Construction of Gender and Sexuality*. Cambridge: Cambridge University.

Overholt, Thomas W.
    1981   "Prophecy: The Problem of Cross-Cultural Comparison." *Semeia* 21: 55–78.
    1982   "Seeing is Believing: The Social Setting of Prophetic Acts of Power." *JSOT* 23: 3–31.
    1989   *Channels of Prophecy: The Social Dynamics of Prophetic Activity*. Minneapolis: Fortress.

Price, Richard
    1983   *First Time: The Historical Vision of an Afro-American People*. Baltimore: Johns Hopkins University

Pritchard, James B. (ed.)
    1950   *Ancient Near Eastern Texts Relating to the Old Testament*. Princeton, N.J.: Princeton University.

Redman, Charles L., Mary J. Berman, Edward V. Curtin, William T. Langhore,Jr., Nina M. Versaggi, J. C. Wanser (eds.)
    1978   *Social Archeology: Beyond Subsistence and Dating*. New York: Academic.

Reeves, Edward B.
    1990   *Hidden Government: Ritual, Clientelism, and Legitimation in Northern Egypt*. Salt Lake City: University of Utah.

Rentería, Tamis Hoover
    1984   "Omride Israel and the Elijah-Elisha Stories: A Systemic Study." Unpublished masters thesis, Graduate Theological Union.

Rofé, Alexander
    1988   *The Prophetical Stories: The Narratives about the Prophets in the Hebrew Bible, Their Literary Types and History*. Jerusalem: Magnes.
    1989   "The Classification of the Prophetical Stories." *JBL* 89: 427–40.

Rosenfeld, Henry
    1972   "An Overview and Critique of the Literature on Rural Politics and Social Change." Pp. 45–74 in *Rural Politics and Social Change in the Middle East*. Ed. R. Antoun and I. Harik. Bloomington: Indiana University.

Rosaldo, Michelle Z.
    1974   "Introduction." Pp. 1–15 in *Woman, Culture, and Society*. Ed. Michelle Z. Rosaldo and Louise Lamphere. Stanford: Stanford University.

Rosaldo, Renato
    1989   *Culture and Truth: The Remaking of Social Analysis*. Boston: Beacon.

Saggs, H. W. F.
    1962   *The Greatness That Was Babylon: A Sketch of the Ancient Civilization of the Tigris Euphrates Valley*. New York: Hawthorne.

Sanders, W. T., and D. Webster
    1978   "Unilinealism, Multilinealism, and the Evolution of Complex Societies." In *Social Archeology: Beyond Subsistence and Dating*. Ed. Redman et al. New York: Academic.

Schaar, Stuart
    1967   "Rebellion, Revolution, and Religious Intermediaries in Some Nineteenth-Century Islamic States." Pp. 121–44 in *Churches and States: The Religious Institution and Modernization*. Ed. Kalman H. Silvert. New York: American Universities Field Staff.

Schaef, Anne Wilson
    1981   *Womens' Reality: An Emerging Female System in the White Male Society*. Minneapolis: Winston.

Scholem, Gershom
    1971   *The Messianic Idea in Judaism*. New York: Schocken.

Scott, James C.
    1985   *Weapons of the Weak: Everyday Forms of Peasant Resistance*. New Haven: Yale University.

Springborg, Robert
    1982   *Family, Power, and Politics in Egypt*. Philadelphia: University of Pennsylvania.

Stager, Lawrence E.
    1976   "Agriculture." Pp. 11-13 in *IDB Supp. Vol.*. Nashville: Abingdon Press.
    1990   "Shemer's Estate." Pp. 93-107 in *BASOR* 277/278: 93–107.

Stevens, John Lloyd
 1839 *Incidents of Travel in Egypt, Arabia Petraea, and the Holy Land.* 2 vols. New York: Harper and Bros.

Tadmor, Hayim
 1975 "Assyria and the West: The Ninth Century and its Aftermath." Pp. 36–48 in *Unity and Diversity: Essays in the History, Literature, and Religion of The Ancient Near East.* Ed. H. Tadmor. Baltimore: Johns Hopkins University.

Taussig, Michael
 1980 *The Devil and Commodity Fetishism In South America.* Chapel Hill: University of North Carolina.

Thompson, E. P.
 1963 *The Making of the English Working Class.* New York: Vintage.
 1978 *The Poverty of Theory.* New York: Monthly Review.

Thompson, Warren, and David Lewis
 1956 *Population Problems.* 5th ed. New York: McGraw-Hill.

Turner, Edith, and Victor Turner
 1978 *Image and Pilgrimage in Christian Culture: Anthropological Perspectives.* New York: Columbia University.

Unger, Merrill F.
 1957 *Israel and the Aramaeans of Damascus.* Grand Rapids: Zondervan.

de Vaux, Roland
 1965 *Ancient Israel,* 2 vols. New York: McGraw-Hill.

Vermes, Geza
 1973 *Jesus the Jew: A Historian's Reading of the Gospels.* London: Collins.
 1981 Philadelphia: Fortress.

Whitelam, Keith W.
 1986 "The Symbols of Power: Aspects of Royal Propaganda in the United Monarchy." *BA* 49: 166–73.
 1989 "Israelite Kingship: The Royal Ideology and its Opponents." Pp. 119–39 in *The World of Ancient Israel.* Ed. R. E. Clements. Cambridge: Cambridge University.

Williams, Raymond
 1966 *Marxism and Literature.* New York: Oxford University.

Willis, Paul
 1977 *Learning to Labor: How Working Class Kids Get Working Class Jobs.* New York: Columbia.

Wilson, Robert R.
    1980   *Prophecy and Society in Ancient Israel.* Philadelphia: Fortress.

Wire, Antoinette Clark
    1978   "The Structure of the Gospel Miracle Stories and Their Tellers." *Semeia* 11: 29–37.
    1981   "The Miracle Story as the Whole Story." *South East Asia Journal of Theology* 22: 29–37.

Wolf, Eric R.
    1966   *Peasants.* Foundations of Modern Anthropology Series. Englewood Cliffs: Prentice-Hall.

al-Yassim, Ayman S.
    1983   "Saudi Arabia: The Kingdom of Islam." Pp. 61–84 in *Religion and Societies: Asia and the Middle East.* Ed. Carlo Caldarola. New York: Mouton.

Zenner, Walter P.
    1972   "Aqiili Agha: The Strongman in the Ethnic Relations of the Ottoman Galilee." *Comparative Studies in Society and History* 14: 169–88.

Subject Index

'Abd el-Qadr, 58
'Abd el-Wahhab, 42
Abu Ghosh, 39, 46
Ahab, 1, 3, 7, 8-12, 16-19, 22, 23, 30, 32-34, 66, 68, 69, 71, 73, 86, 87, 89, 93, 94, 95, 119, 123, 127, 134
Ahaziah, 3, 30-31, 87, 94, 134
Ahmad al Badawi, 39, 53
Al-Azhar University, 50
'Ali Matar, 49
Ambrose, 56, 58, 63
Amos, 125
Aphek, 86
Aqiili Agha, 45, 50, 55
Ashera, 91
Asshur-nasir-pal II, 85, 86
Avihatsira, Israel (Baba Sali), 61

Baal, 1, 10, 11, 15-16, 19, 21-23, 25, 26, 66, 67, 71, 76, 91, 96, 113, 122, 123, 135
Baal-zebub, 30-31
Baasha, 35
Bab, 55, 69
Baha'ullah, 55, 69
Ben-hadad, 24, 30-31, 86, 87
Bethel, 28, 98

Carmel, 16, 23, 64, 65, 67, 70, 71

Damascus, 30, 65, 85, 86, 87
Daniel, 60
David, 4, 10, 32, 65, 84, 88
Dervishes, 55
Deuteronomist, xii, 1, 38-39, 40, 45, 51, 58, 64, 65-66, 67, 69, 73, 112, 125, 127-29, 131-34, 136
Dothan, 132, 136

Ekron, 30-31
El-Khadr, 64, 72
Esh-Sheikh el-Qatrawani, 59

Gehazi, 104-7, 115
George, Saint, 64
Gervasius, Saint, 50, 56-57
Gilead, 65, 66, 70, 73, 87, 120, 136
Gilgal, 28

Ha-Moshe, David, 62
Hanina ben Dosa, 57
Hazael, x, 2, 27, 30-31, 133
Hegemony, 79-82, 113, 120, 124, 125, 126
Hezekiah, 71

"High places," 42
Honi the Circle-drawer, 43, 53, 54, 56, 57, 62, 66
Horeb, 3, 10, 11, 23-27, 69
Hosea, 125

Ibrahim Barham, 49
Igurramen, 59-60
Irhuleni, 87
Israel, 61
Ittoba'al, 86

Jacob, 21
James, 51
Jehonadab ben Recheb, 89
Jehoram, *see* Joram
Jehoshaphat, 130, 134
Jehu, ix, x, xi, 1, 2, 3, 10, 11, 19, 26, 27, 31-35, 37, 38, 65, 66, 68, 69, 70, 71, 73, 77, 80, 81, 87, 89, 92, 95, 96, 104, 118, 119, 120, 121, 123, 125, 126
Jericho, 28
Jeroboam, 4, 34, 85
Jesus, 42, 49, 51-52, 53, 54, 55, 57, 59, 62, 64, 69
Jezebel, 1, 9, 10, 11, 17, 18, 22-25, 32-35, 67, 73, 86, 91, 123, 124, 127
Jezreel, 8, 16, 22, 27, 31-34, 65, 89, 90, 104
Joahaz, x
Joash, x
John the Baptizer, 55, 62, 64, 69
Joram, 1, 3, 7, 10, 31, 32, 34, 70, 87, 94, 130, 134
Jordan, 28-29, 58, 70
Josephus, 7
Joshua, 19, 23, 28-29, 55, 69
Josiah, 71

Khaddam, 44
Khidrlas, 72

Laurel Lady, 43
Local hero, definition, 39-40, 46, 52

Mahdi, 62-63
Maqam, 43
Mawlid, 43
Menander, 7
Meron, 62
Mexico, 99
Micaiah, 12
Mohammed ibn 'Abd el-Wahhab, 49, 50-51
Mohammed Ahmed, 63
Morocco, 40, 50, 61-62, 68
Moses, x, xii, 11, 23, 25, 26, 28-29, 35, 39, 46, 55, 58, 67, 68, 69, 119, 128, 130
Muhammad al-Jazuli, 68
Musa as-Sadr, 42, 47-48, 50, 55, 63

Naaman, 70, 131
Nabi Musa, 63
Nabi Rubain, 63
Nabi Yamin, 63
Naboth, 2, 8-9, 27, 32-34, 68, 90-91, 96
Nathan of Gaza, 55, 69

Oath, 43-44
Obadiah, 17-19, 23, 30
Omri, Omrids, ix, x, xi, 1, 3-11, 32, 35, 37, 38, 73, 75-78, 80, 81, 82, 83-95, 96, 101, 102, 109, 113-25

Pekah, 65
Pharisees, 54, 57
Protasius, Saint, 50, 56-57

Qarqar, 87

Rachel, 98, 105
Ramoth-Gilead, 68, 69, 87
Rashid ed-Din Sinan, 53-54
Rehoboam, 4

Samaria, 16, 17, 30, 32-33, 89, 90-91, 93, 104, 132, 133, 136
Saudi Arabia, 50-51
Saul, 10, 11, 84

Shabbetai Zevi, 50, 53, 54, 55, 69
Shalmaneser III, 87, 93
Shechem, 98
Shishak, 86
Shunammite woman, 9, 104-8, 114, 116, 118, 132
Shunem, 91, 104
Sibleh, 45
Solomon, 4, 84, 88, 93
Sozomen, 48

Temple, 38
Tirzah, 89
Tishbe, 136
Tyre, 85, 8691

Wely, xi, 39, 41, 44, 46, 50, 58, 60, 61, 63, 72

Zarephath, 13, 15, 17, 65, 117
Zechariah, 51

Author Index

Aharoni, Y., 85
Ajami, F., 47, 48
Albright, W. F., 31
Alt, A., 4, 11
Althusser, L., 79
Andersen, F. I., 33
Augustinovic, A., 72
Avi-Yonah, M., 85

Bailey, F. G., 78, 82, 109, 110, 120
Bal, M., 129
Baldensperger, P. J., 42, 53, 58
Bergen, W. J., xii
Bourdieu, P., 79
Bright, J., 4, 10, 78, 93, 94
Brown, J. P., 55
Brown, P., 48, 55, 56, 59, 63
Burney, C. F., 28

Campbell, A. F., 11
Canaan, T., 42, 43, 44, 58, 59, 60, 67
Carlson, R. A., 21, 25, 26, 30
Carroll, R. P., 28, 29
Chaney, M. L., 4, 7, 9, 76, 78, 85, 89, 90, 93, 111, 120
Clifford, J., 83
Cohen, A., 49, 63

Cohen, G. A., 79
Cohen, M. A., 33
Cohen, R., 84
Collier, J. F., 82, 105
Comaroff, J., 78, 81, 122
Conder, C. R., 42, 46, 58
Coote, M. P., 78
Coote, R. B., 23, 25, 27, 78, 91
Corrington, G. P., 58
Cross, F. M., 10, 12, 22, 25, 26, 31, 91

Foucault, M., 129
Frank, H. T., 85
Fried, M., 84
Frick, F. S., 78

Geertz, C., 79, 83
Gellner, E., 42, 58, 59, 60
Gilsenan, M., 39
Goldberg, H., 43, 44, 61-62
Gottwald, N. K., 4, 8, 10, 78, 105, 110
Grant, E., 42
Gray, J., 10, 31, 96, 104
Green, W. S., 57, 62
Greenstein, E., x, xii
Guillaume, A., 63

Hanauer, J. E., 42
Harris, M., 92, 93, 94, 95
Hayes, J. H., 134
Hill, S. D., x-xi, 75, 81, 82, 97, 104, 118, 121
Hooker, P. K., 134

Josephus, 7

Kapferer, B., 78
Kenyon, K., 32
Kolenkow, A., 58

Lenski, G., 3, 5, 6, 7, 9, 86, 90, 92, 93
Lenski, J., 3, 5
Lewis, D., 108, 113
Long, B. O., 30
Luke, H., 42, 54

Macalister, R. A., 42, 55, 58
Maddin, R., 85
Malamat, A., 31
Marsot, A. L. al-S., 50
Masterman, E. W. G., 42, 55, 58
Mazar, B., 31
Miller, E., 98
Miller, J. M., 32, 33, 34, 35
Montgomery, J. A., 96
Moore, B., 95
Muhly, J. D., 85

Napier, B. D., 32, 89, 90
Niditch, S., 105, 106
Noel, D. C., 99

Ortner, S. B., 79
Overholt, T. W., 39, 40, 41

Price, R., 81
Pritchard, J. B., 31

Reeves, E. B., xi

Renteria, T. H., x, xi-xii, 37, 45, 66, 71, 98
Rofé, A., ix, x, xi, 96
Rosaldo, M. Z., 79, 82
Rosaldo, R., 79, 83

Saggs, H. W. F., 87
Schaar, S., 45, 62
Schaef, A. W., 46
Scholem, G., 53
Scott, J. C., 81
Stager, L. E., 6, 89

Tadmor, H., 87
Taussig, M., 81
Thompson, E. P., 79, 80
Thompson, W., 108, 113
Todd, J. A., ix-x, 37, 66, 68, 69, 77, 89, 90, 91, 92, 93, 119, 121, 123

Unger, M. F., 31

de Vaux, R., 8
Vermes, G., 54, 57, 62

Weir, B., 47
Weir, C., 47
Wheeler, T. S., 85
Whitehead, H., 79
Whitelam, K. W., 92
Williams, R., 79, 80, 124
Willis, P., 79
Wilson, R. R., 34, 35, 97, 119
Wire, A. C., 98, 100, 110
Wolf, E. R., 5, 7, 26, 93, 94, 97

al-Yassim, A. S., 50

Zenner, W. P., 46, 55

www.ingramcontent.com/pod-product-compliance
Lightning Source LLC
Chambersburg PA
CBHW021811220426
43662CB00006B/272